Israel and the Arab States

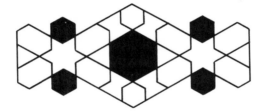

Richard Worth

A GROLIER COMPANY

FRANKLIN WATTS
NEW YORK | LONDON
TORONTO | SYDNEY | 1983
AN IMPACT BOOK

Maps, pp. 22 and 49 courtesy of Vantage Art, Inc.

Library of Congress Cataloging in Publication Data
Worth, Richard.
Israel and the Arab states.

(An Impact book)
Bibliography: p.
Includes index.
Summary: Describes the history of relations between
Israel and her Arab neighbors, including the peace
talks and treaty between Egypt's Sadat and Israel.
1. Jewish-Arab relations—1917-   —Juvenile literature.
2. Israel-Arab War, 1973—Peace—Juvenile literature.
3. Israel—Foreign relations—Egypt—Juvenile literature.
4. Egypt—Foreign relations—Israel—Juvenile literature.
[1. Jewish-Arab relations. 2. Israel—Foreign relations—Egypt.
3. Egypt—Foreign relations—Israel]   I. Title.
DS119.7.W73 1983   956   82-20315
ISBN 0-531-04545-5

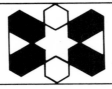

Contents

INTRODUCTION
1

CHAPTER 1
NEXT YEAR IN JERUSALEM
3

CHAPTER 2
WAR! 1948
17

CHAPTER 3
CRISIS AT SUEZ
25

CHAPTER 4
SIX DAYS IN JUNE
38

CHAPTER 5
YOM KIPPUR, 1973
52

CHAPTER 6
SADAT, BEGIN, AND CARTER
66

CHAPTER 7
WILL THERE BE PEACE?
78

FOR FURTHER READING
85

INDEX
87

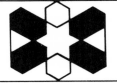

Israel
and the
Arab
States

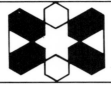

Introduction

In August 1977, an important meeting took place outside Bucharest, the capital of Rumania. Present at the meeting were Israeli Prime Minister Menachem Begin and Rumania's President Nicolae Ceausescu. Begin reportedly told the Rumanian leader that the Israelis were interested in peace with Egypt and would return the Sinai Peninsula—Egyptian territory which Israel had conquered during the 1967 war—in order to secure a treaty. Since the Israelis did not maintain diplomatic relations with Egypt, Begin hoped Ceausescu would see that this information was transmitted to the Egyptian government.

After Begin returned, peace discussions continued in September at a secret meeting of Egyptian and Israeli representatives in Morocco. Unlike many other Arab states, the Moroccan government of King Hassan II had never taken an extreme position against Israel. In fact earlier that year, when Israeli intelligence had discovered a Libyan plot against the life of Egyptian president Anwar el-Sadat, the Israelis had passed the information along via Morocco. This gesture had been greatly appreciated by the Egyptians.

In October, President Sadat traveled to Bucharest for a meeting with Ceausescu. During their conversations, the Rumanian leader apparently told Sadat that "Begin wants a solution."

After his visit, Sadat said an idea came to him that might break down the "psychological barrier" separating Egypt and Israel. Later, in a speech before the Egyptian parliament, Sadat announced that he was prepared to go to Jerusalem and speak before the Knesset—the Israeli parliament—if that would secure peace.

Prime Minister Begin was taken by surprise at Sadat's announcement. No Arab leader had ever made such a proposal. Nevertheless he extended an invitation for Sadat to address the Knesset. Throughout much of the Arab world, on the other hand, Sadat was loudly denounced. Arabs branded him a traitor for planning to set foot on Israeli soil and talk peace with their long-time enemy.

On November 19, 1977, Anwar Sadat risked his position of leadership in the Arab world and made an historic visit to Jerusalem. He became the first Egyptian president ever to speak before the Knesset:

> *I come to you today on solid ground to shape a new life and establish peace.*
>
> *We all still bear the consequences of four fierce wars waged within thirty years. . . . Any life that is lost in war is a human life, be it that of an Arab or an Israeli.*
>
> *Ring the bells for your sons. Tell them that those wars were the last of wars and the end of sorrows. Tell them that we are entering upon a new beginning, a new life, a life of love, prosperity, freedom, and peace.*

Sadat's visit electrified the world. It also signified an important step on the road to peace in a region which had known little else but conflict.

[2]

1

Next Year in Jerusalem

On the eastern shore of the Mediterranean Sea lies the area known historically as Palestine. It is often called the Holy Land because of its importance to three great religions.

The Jews migrated to Palestine during the second millenium B.C. and established their splendid capital at Jerusalem. Palestine was also the birthplace of Jesus Christ. He was born in Bethlehem, preached in many parts of the Holy Land, and died on the cross at Jerusalem.

The city of Jerusalem has special meaning to Muslims too. It is here that Mohammed, the Prophet of Islam, is believed to have ascended into heaven. After they conquered Palestine in the seventh century A.D., the Arabs built a shrine, called the Dome of the Rock, over the rock from which the Prophet is said to have made his ascent.

Thus the region of Palestine is sacred to Jews, Christians, and Muslims. It is also considered a homeland by Arabs and Jews. These historical factors help explain the conflict between Israel and the Arab states that exists in the Middle East today.

[3]

THE JEWS AND PALESTINE

To the Jews, Palestine is their ancient homeland. In the Old Testament of the Bible, God promised the Patriarch Abraham the land of Canaan, roughly ancient Palestine. According to the Book of Genesis, God said to Abraham: "I will make a great nation of you. . . . To your descendants I will give this land."

The Bible explains that Abraham left his home and traveled to the land of Canaan, to the Negev Desert, into Egypt, and to other places as well. It remained for later generations to actually occupy the promised land. Centuries after Abraham's death, Moses led the Israelites out of bondage in Egypt, and his successor, Joshua, finally brought them to glorious triumph in Palestine. At the battle of Jericho, for example, the Bible says that Joshua ordered the Israelites to shout and their trumpets to sound. Then the walls of the city collapsed, and the Israelites stormed it. Joshua conquered much of Palestine, defeating the local tribes who were ancient ancestors of the Arabs.

Under the leadership of two great kings (about 1010 to 930 B.C.), the territory of the Israelites expanded. King David defeated the Philistines along the Mediterranean coast and captured Jerusalem from the Jebasites. His son Solomon enlarged the kingdom. King Solomon also built a splendid temple in Jerusalem, which is known as the First Temple.

After the death of Solomon, the power of the Israelites declined. Solomon's realm was split into two kingdoms, Israel in the north and Judah, with its capital at Jerusalem, in the south. During this period the Biblical prophets criticized the inhabitants of Judah and Israel because of their sinfulness and warned that they would be punished. Punishment came with the armies of the Assyrians, who captured Israel in the eighth century B.C.

Less than two centuries later, it was Judah's turn. In 586 B.C., the Babylonian King Nebuchadnezzar captured Jerusalem, destroyed the Temple, and led the Jews into

[4]

captivity. This event marks the beginning of the Jewish Diaspora, or dispersion. But, even though they had been exiled, the Jews never forgot their homeland, and they vowed to return. Psalm 137 states:

By the waters of Babylon,
There we sat down and wept,
When we remembered Zion [the Jewish home-
land].
. . . .
How shall we sing the Lord's song
In a foreign land?
If I forget you, O Jerusalem,
Let my right hand wither!
Let my tongue cleave to the roof
Of my mouth,
If I do not remember you,
If I do not set Jerusalem
Above my highest joy!

A few decades later, the Persian King Cyrus the Great conquered the Babylonian empire and allowed the Jews to go home. Some returned and rebuilt the Temple, which remained for centuries until the conquest of the Romans. The Jews did not submit easily to the domination of Rome, and they revolted in A.D. 64. The bloody revolt was finally put down by the Emperor Titus who burned the Temple in A.D. 70 and destroyed Jerusalem. Most of the Jews fled Palestine and began another Diaspora that would last almost two thousand years.

During their long Diaspora, the Jews migrated to many parts of the known world. In western Europe, they met with persecution by Christians who treated them as second-class citizens. Jews were prohibited from owning land and therefore often became usurers, or moneylenders, an occupation closed to Christians by the Catholic Church. In towns and cities, Jews were confined to special areas called ghettoes. Even this policy did not seem

[5]

severe enough to some medieval rulers, who went so far as to expel the Jews from their countries. Jews were forced out of England and France during the fourteenth century. After the Christians reconquered Spain from the Arabs in 1492, the Jews were given a choice between exile or Christian baptism, resulting in a mass Jewish exodus.

Under the Arabs, whose empire during the Middle Ages stretched from Asia across North Africa and into Spain, the Jews generally fared better. They enjoyed more autonomy than the Jews of western Christendom and participated more extensively in the cultural life of the empire. During the tenth century in Spain, for example, Jews and Arabs created a golden age in philosophy, literature, and biblical studies.

Despite the fact that they were scattered throughout the world and often lived in very different circumstances, the Jewish people still retained a sense of unity. This was due to their common heritage and religion as well as their strong sense of identity in being Jews. The Jewish people believed they had been chosen by God to fulfill a special destiny. That destiny included exile and suffering. But one day the exile would end, and the Jews would return to their homeland.

Suddenly, in the nineteenth century, a series of events occurred which seemed to fulfill the Jewish destiny.

THE POWER OF ZIONISM
The French Revolution of 1789 unleashed the forces of liberty, equality, and nationalism across the map of Europe. During the nineteenth century, as a result of the revolution, restrictions against Jews in France and other western European states were gradually lifted. But there was a price: assimilation. Jews were expected to give up their separatism (a kind of nationalism), become like other Europeans, and blend into society. They had to

abandon at least the public display of their beliefs, including the goal of returning to their ancient homeland. Many Jews chose the path of assimilation, hoping that at last they might be accepted by European society.

The spirit of liberty and equality took far longer to penetrate the rigid society of eastern Europe. Only in the latter part of the nineteenth century, for example, did Tsar Alexander II attempt to improve the position of the Jews in Russia. Then in 1881, the tsar was assassinated. The Jews, always a convenient scapegoat, were thought to be somehow responsible. They became victims of a terrible wave of violent persecutions that swept over the Russian empire.

Many Jews were now convinced that liberty—and equality—were forever impossible in the Russian empire, and assimilation therefore could never be achieved. Beginning in 1882, Jews from Russia and Rumania began to leave eastern Europe to start a new life in an ancient Jewish homeland, Palestine. Over the next two decades, twenty-five thousand Jewish settlers came to Palestine. This is called the first Aliyah (loosely translated, "wave of migration").

In the same year that the first Aliyah began, a Russian Jew named Leon Pinsker published a pamphlet called *Auto-emancipation: A Warning of a Russian Jew to His Brethren*. In the pamphlet Pinsker called for the establishment of a Jewish state. With the publication of this pamphlet and the Jewish migration to Palestine, the movement known as Zionism—the desire for a Jewish national homeland—was now firmly under way. Zionism arose from different sources. In part it represented a resurgence of the ancient longing of the Jews to return to Palestine. But the movement was also rooted in the nationalism unleashed by the French Revolution and in the persecutions the Jews had suffered in Russia.

The cause of Zionism was later taken up by a Hungarian-born Jew named Theodor Herzl. In 1895 Herzl was a journalist covering the Dreyfus Affair in France. Alfred Dreyfus had served as an artillery officer on the General Staff of the French Army. He was relieved of his duties after being accused of passing military secrets to the Germans. Although Dreyfus was innocent, he was a Jew and seemed like the perfect scapegoat. His trial touched off a huge outcry of anti-Semitism, and he was convicted, stripped of his rank, and sent off to prison. The Dreyfus Affair apparently had a great impact on Theodor Herzl. It convinced him that the Jews could never be assimilated into the society of western Europe.

In 1896 Herzl published a book proposing the creation of a Jewish state. The following year he convened the First Zionist Congress in Basle, Switzerland. At the conclusion of the congress, he wrote:

In Basle I founded the Jewish State. If I were to say this aloud I would meet with general laughter; but in another five years, and certainly in another fifty years, everyone will be convinced of this.

Although many Jews in Europe believed in assimilation, Herzl succeeded in convincing a few of the need for a Jewish homeland. One of these was Baron Edmond de Rothschild, a member of the famous family of international bankers. Herzl persuaded Rothschild to purchase land in Palestine for Jewish settlers. For his efforts on behalf of the Jewish homeland, Rothschild has been called the "father of the Yishuv" (the Jewish community in Palestine).

Jewish settlers arrived in Palestine expecting the land there to be completely unoccupied. To their amazement, they encountered Arab peasant farmers, *fellahin,* who had lived in Palestine for centuries. The Arabs

[8]

regarded Palestine as theirs, and they did not want to share it with a group of Jewish settlers. Although in some cases Arab and Jew were able to live together peacefully, many of the fellahin regarded these immigrants with disfavor. In turn, the Jews often made little or no attempt to understand the customs of the Arabs. Under these circumstances friction became inevitable. Conflicts also arose because the land purchased for the Jewish immigrants was often taken from the fellahin unfairly and under the threat of force.

Some of the Zionist leaders were distressed about removing the Arabs from their land. As Max Nordan, an associate of Herzl's, put it: "But there are Arabs in Palestine. I didn't know that. We're committing an injustice."

Nevertheless the Jewish immigration continued. During the second Aliyah, 1904–1914, forty thousand Jewish settlers arrived. At this time, the Jews established their first kibbutz. This was a commune, or collective, in which all the land was held in common and worked together. In the kibbutz, European Jews, who had little or no experience on farms, could be trained for agricultural work. Gradually they learned how to tend the fields and plant the vineyards.

Meanwhile, friction between Jew and Arab had not diminished. Many of the Arabs were inspired by the same spirit of nationalism which had swept across Europe. Since the sixteenth century they had been subject people, ruled by the Ottoman Turks. But by 1914, the Turkish empire was crumbling and the Arabs wanted desperately to remove its yoke and reassert their independence. Like the Jews, the Arabs of Palestine regarded this land as their home and they hoped to secure it for themselves. Some observers remarked at the time that the aspirations of Arab and Jew in Palestine were on a collision course that would eventually result in bloody conflict.

[9]

THE IMPACT OF WORLD WAR I

In 1914 the assassination of Austrian Archduke Franz Ferdinand touched off the First World War in Europe. Turkey fought alongside Germany and Austria-Hungary against the Allies—France, Russia, and Great Britain. In an effort to weaken the Turkish empire and eventually knock it out of the war, Britain tried to instigate a revolt among the Arabs. During 1915, negotiations proceeded between the British and Sharif Hussein of the Hejaz, an Arab leader. Hussein explained that the Arabs were prepared to attack the Turks, but in return Britain must be willing to recognize an independent Arab state. This state would stretch from Persia and the Persian Gulf westward to the shores of the Mediterranean Sea, with Hussein as its king.

After an agreement had been concluded, Hussein's revolt began. To advise the Arabs, the British sent in one of their officers, T. E. Lawrence. A dashing figure who seemed at home in the desert, Lawrence rode with the Arabs as they attacked Turkish supply depots and disrupted their communications. The Arab sorties proved very effective in tying down Turkish troops that might have been used against the British during their march into Palestine. For his daring exploits, Lawrence was given the romantic title "Lawrence of Arabia."

While the British government fought side by side with the Arabs, it was also strengthening its ties with the Jews. On November 2, 1917, British Foreign Secretary Arthur Balfour issued the following statement in a letter to Lord Rothschild:

> *Dear Lord Rothschild,*
> *I have much pleasure in conveying to you, on behalf of His Majesty's Government, the following declaration of sympathy with Jewish Zionist aspirations which has been submitted to, and approved by the Cabinet.*

[10]

"His Majesty's Government view with favor the establishment in Palestine of a national home for the Jewish people, and will use their best endeavors to facilitate the achievement of this object, it being clearly understood that nothing shall be done which may prejudice the civil and religious rights of existing non-Jewish communities in Palestine, or the rights and political status enjoyed by Jews in any other country."

This statement became known as the famous Balfour Declaration, promising a home to the Jews. Why did the British choose this moment to issue the declaration? Their motives were political as well as humanitarian. In 1917 a revolution had engulfed Russia, and a new government had come to power which might have taken Russia out of the war. The British hoped the declaration would find favor with Russian Jews who were thought to have influence with the new government and could persuade it to keep fighting. In 1917 the United States had entered the war on the side of the Allies. Britain felt the declaration might please American Jews and help cement the alliance. The British also acted out of humanitarian reasons, believing the Jews were entitled to a national homeland. Finally Britain wanted to show its gratitude to Zionist leader Dr. Chaim Weizmann. He was a chemist who had helped the British develop a new process for manufacturing explosives.

While the Zionists were pleased with the Balfour Declaration, it angered the Arab leader Sharif Hussein. He believed the British had violated their agreement to recognize an independent Arab state. How could this state and the Jewish national home occupy some of the same territory? But the British told him that Jewish settlement would be permitted only "insofar as would be consistent with the . . . freedom of the Arab population."

[11]

A short time later Hussein learned of the secret Sykes-Picot agreement between Britain and France. According to its terms, the two powers planned to divide up many of the Arab lands between themselves. But, once more, the British reassured him that this would not prevent them from honoring their commitments to the Arabs.

By war's end, Great Britain had made three separate agreements—with the Arabs, the Jews, and the French. Each party expected Britain to fulfill its agreement. Yet each agreement contradicted the other. Thus it would be impossible for Britain to carry out all of them.

BETWEEN THE WARS

At the peace conference following World War I, the victorious Allies destroyed Hussein's plans for an independent Arab state encompassing Lebanon, Syria, Iraq and Palestine. Instead the League of Nations gave France mandates (i.e. effective control) over Lebanon and Syria, while Great Britain was given mandates over Iraq and Palestine. (See map, p. 22.) The Palestinian mandate gave special attention to the interests of the Jews. It recognized the "historical connection of the Jewish people with Palestine" and encouraged Jewish immigration to the region. As Balfour explained:

> *In Palestine we do not propose even to go through the form of consulting the wishes of the present inhabitants of the country. . . . the four Great Powers are committed to Zionism.*

Beginning in 1919 the Jewish community, which had shrunk during the war, increased again as more immigrants arrived in Palestine. By 1925 there were over one hundred thousand Jews, and their settlements had grown as they had continued purchasing land from the Arabs.

[12]

Many of the seven hundred thousand Arabs in Palestine regarded the Jewish presence as a grave threat to their homeland. In 1921 the Arabs staged bloody riots as a protest against the Jews. There were burnings and killings in Jerusalem, Jaffa, and other cities. The British tried to reduce the violence by issuing a white paper in 1922. This limited Jewish immigration in Palestine and shut off to the Jews the area east of the Jordan, called Transjordan. Jewish leaders protested that the white paper had violated the Balfour Declaration.

The Arabs were not satisfied with British policy either. Arab riots broke out in 1929. This time over one hundred Jews and almost as many Arabs lost their lives. A report issued by a British commission investigating the riots stated that the Arabs believed continued immigration of Jews would lead to a Jewish majority in Palestine. The commission recommended that immigration once again be restricted. Yet, as the Nazis increased their power in Europe during the 1930s, the Jews were forced to flee and many were permitted to enter Palestine.

In 1936 Arab dissatisfaction over continued Jewish immigration and land purchases broke out into full-scale rebellion. At this point the British declared that their mandate was no longer workable. They proposed instead that Palestine be partitioned into an Arab state and a Jewish state. A majority of Jews were prepared to accept partition under certain conditions, but the Arabs opposed it. To them partition meant that the Jews, who now controlled only a small part of Palestine, would be given much more.

The conflict in Palestine continued. Arab battled Jew as well as the British army of occupation. To combat the Arabs, the British even began training some members of the Haganah, a military force established by the Jews to defend themselves. Finally, the violence was reduced, but only after many Arabs had been killed, arrested, or deported. Yet the Arabs had succeeded in preventing partition.

[13]

Throughout its mandate in Palestine, Britain seemed to follow a policy of vacillation. It supported the Jews, then tried to restrict immigration to appease the Arabs, and finally worked with the Jewish Haganah during the last crisis. As another world war approached in 1939, British policy changed once again. The fascist dictatorships of Germany and Italy were busy intriguing among the Arabs to set them against Great Britain. The British feared that their interests in the Middle East might be jeopardized and that the flow of oil, which was Britain's lifeline, could be cut off. The British government was, therefore, eager to satisfy Arab demands in Palestine.

In 1939, British leaders met in London with representatives of the Zionists, the Palestinian Arabs, and other Arab leaders to discuss the Palestinian situation. No agreements were reached. Britain then issued another white paper, saying that it would continue to govern Palestine for ten more years. After that period, if Jews and Arabs could cooperate, an independent state would be created. Meanwhile Jewish immigration and land purchases would be severely limited.

The white paper was strongly opposed by the Jews, who said it would lead to an Arab state in Palestine. But this problem seemed far less important to the British than the need for Arab support in the coming war.

WORLD WAR II AND THE
PARTITION OF PALESTINE

During World War II approximately forty-three thousand Palestinian Jews fought with the British against the Axis powers. While the Jews did not agree with Britain's policy in Palestine, they did support efforts to defeat the Nazis, who were slaughtering millions of Jewish people throughout Europe. The British trained members of the Haganah and eventually organized a Jewish brigade. Yet, even in the face of Nazi persecutions, the British immigration policy in Palestine remained unchanged. The few refugee ships that escaped the Holocaust were not allowed to enter Palestine. Nevertheless, some Jews were successfully smuggled into the country.

In 1944, after the Axis threat to the Middle East had receded, Jewish groups mounted guerrilla attacks against the British administration in Palestine. Menachem Begin, leader of a radical Zionist group called the Irgun, issued the following statement:

> *There is no longer any armistice between the Jewish people and the British Administration in Eretz Israel which hands our brothers over to Hitler. . . . This, then is our demand: immediate transfer of power in Eretz Israel to a Provisional Hebrew Government.*

After the war had ended, the full extent of Nazi atrocities against the Jews became public. The British then found themselves under increasing pressure from the United States and world Jewry to admit more Jewish refugees to Palestine. At the same time, the Arabs warned that they would not allow Palestine to be turned into a Jewish state, and Britain feared that, by antagonizing the Arabs, its interests in the Middle East would be jeopardized.

Since the British refused to change their policy, the Jews increasingly took matters into their own hands. Inside Palestine, guerrilla activities increased. In July 1946, the Irgun attacked the offices of the British administration at the King David Hotel in Jerusalem. This act of terror cost many civil servants their lives and left many others wounded. At the same time, the Haganah was attempting to bring thousands of Jewish refugees out of Europe and transport them illegally into Palestine. However, many of the refugee ships, including the famous *Exodus,* were turned back.

[15]

By the beginning of 1947, the situation in Palestine had reached a crisis. The Jews now numbered about six hundred thousand or one-third of the population. They were demanding an independent state, at least in part of the area. The Arabs, on the other hand, had vowed to oppose any plan that called for a partition of Palestine and the continuation of Jewish immigration. Realizing that they could never bring the two sides to an agreement, the British decided to let the United Nations find a solution for Palestine.

On November 29, 1947, the General Assembly of the United Nations passed a resolution calling for the partition of Palestine. It had the vigorous support of the United States and the Soviet Union. The partition plan set up an Arab state including the eastern portion of Palestine, the southern Mediterranean coast, and part of northern Palestine. A Jewish state, somewhat larger, would include the coastal region from Haifa to the Tel Aviv area, eastern Galilee, and most of the Negev. The two states would be linked together by an economic union, and Jerusalem would be an international zone. These two states would replace the British mandate no later than October 1948. (See map, p. 22.)

The struggle for Palestine now intensified.

2

War!
1948

On May 14, 1948, David Ben-Gurion, Israel's first prime minister, made the following announcement from Tel Aviv:

In the Land of Israel the Jewish People came into being. Here they lived in sovereign independence.

Exiled by force, still the Jewish People kept faith with their land in all the countries of their dispersion. . . .

Fired by this attachment of history and tradition, the Jews in every generation strove to renew their roots in the ancient Homeland, and in recent generations they came home in their multitudes.

In 1897 the First Zionist Congress . . . gave public voice to the right of the Jewish People to national restoration in their Land.

This right was acknowledged in the Balfour

*Declaration . . . and confirmed in the Man-
date of the League of Nations. . . .*

*On November 29, 1947, the General Assembly
of the United Nations adopted a resolution
calling for the establishment of a Jewish State
in the Land of Israel. . . .*

*Accordingly we . . . do hereby proclaim the
establishment of the Jewish State in the Land
of Israel—the State of Israel.*

When Israel declared its independence, five months ahead of the October deadline, it was a day of triumph for the Jewish people. At last they had a national state. Yet the triumph was mixed with a sense of deep sadness and grave foreboding, for even as Ben-Gurion spoke, Israel was being ripped apart by a violent war. It was a continuation of the long conflict between Arab and Jew, which had intensified after the UN General Assembly voted for partition in November.

The new Jewish state created by the UN proved very difficult for the Jews to defend. Areas with a high concentration of Jewish settlers were separated from each other by Arab settlements. During 1947–48, the Arabs set about disrupting Jewish lines of communications, attacking *kibbutzim* (plural of *kibbutz*) and terrorizing the Jewish quarters of larger towns. The British, who remained in Palestine until May 1948, when they ended their mandate, made little attempt to stop the Arab attacks.

By March 1948, there were estimated to be a few thousand Arab guerrillas operating in Palestine. Some were poorly organized groups of fellahin. Others were members of the more highly disciplined Palestine Liberation Army. These consisted of volunteers from Palestine and other Arab states trained and equipped by the Arab League. The League, created in 1945 to stop Zionism,

[18]

included the states of Egypt, Syria, Iraq, Transjordan, Saudi Arabia, and Yemen.

At first the Haganah was too poorly equipped to beat the Arabs. Then the Jews began receiving gun shipments from the Soviet bloc. The USSR, which had supported the partition plan, apparently believed that an independent Jewish state would reduce British power and prestige in the Middle East. With their new equipment, the Haganah went on the offensive. They succeeded in opening the road between Tel Aviv and Jerusalem which had been blocked by the Arabs. Jewish forces defeated the Arabs in Haifa, and they took control of Jaffa and Acre, two cities which the UN had not designated as part of Israel.

The series of Jewish victories alarmed the leaders of the Arab world. At a meeting in April 1948, the Arab League ministers decided to invade Palestine. The League members operated from a variety of motives. Some wanted simply to free Palestine from the Jews and return it to the Arabs. Transjordan wanted to annex Israeli territory. Arab League Secretary-General Abd al-Rahman Pasha expressed still another reason for the attack: "This will be a war of extermination and a momentous massacre which will be spoken of like the Mongolian massacres and the Crusades."

THE COURSE OF WAR

On May 15, 1948—the day after Israeli independence—the Arab invasion began. Lebanon attacked from the north, Syria from the northeast, Iraq and the Arab Legion of Transjordan from the east, and Egypt from the South. The Arab forces numbered between twenty and twenty-four thousand. Although better equipped than the Israelis, the Arabs lacked a central command structure, which prevented coordination between their armies.

As the war began, the strength of the Israeli army

was about thirty thousand effective troops. Many of its soldiers had been well trained by the British and combat hardened during World War II. The Israelis had the advantage of interior lines. That is, it was easier for them to move their troops around Israel's defensive perimeter than for the Arabs to coordinate their armies along the wide arc stretching from Lebanon to Egypt. In addition the Israelis possessed the unified and established command structure of the Haganah. They were also fighting for survival, unlike the Arab states. Finally, the Israeli war effort was led by a man of tremendous will and determination, David Ben-Gurion.

As the war opened, the Syrians scored initial victories in the north. Their tanks and artillery proved more than a match for the Israelis, who were lacking in heavy equipment. In a desperate effort to save the situation, a young officer named Moshe Dayan was sent to the northern front. With a few artillery pieces he had managed to collect, Dayan helped rally the Israeli soldiers and forced the Syrians to retreat.

To the south, the Arab Legion had achieved much greater success in its assault on the Jewish controlled section of Jerusalem. The Legion cut off the Old City and eventually forced the Israeli defenders there to surrender. But in the New City, the Legion met stiff resistance, and many areas changed hands again and again. The Egyptians, meanwhile, were approaching Jerusalem from the south, cutting off most of the Negev. Egyptian forces also advanced along the coast toward Tel Aviv, but here they were slowed by the stubborn defense of Israeli kibbutzim and eventually pushed back.

On June 11, Arabs and Israelis began a truce in Palestine under the auspices of the United Nations. Israel welcomed the cease-fire. The army had been hard-pressed on all fronts, and the Israeli soldiers were exhausted. Israel used the armistice period, which lasted for about a month, to rebuild its armed forces. New immigrants, arriving constantly from Europe, were pressed into service. Delivery had already begun in May on equipment from the Communist bloc countries. In fact, Czech fighter planes were used against the Egyptians during their advance on Tel Aviv. In July, when the war resumed, the Israeli army was much improved and numbered about sixty thousand, far more than the Arab forces.

Israel now went on the offensive and never lost the battlefield initiative until the war ended in 1949. The Arab Legion was pushed back from its positions around Jerusalem, although the Israelis failed to break through to the Old City. In the north, Israeli forces took most of central Galilee. Following another truce, fighting continued in October between Israel and Egypt. The Israelis eventually succeeded in driving Egyptian forces out of the Negev and capturing the port of Eilat, at the head of the Gulf of Aqaba, which gave Israel access to the Red Sea. As 1948 ended, Israeli forces drove farther into Egypt, but they were eventually stopped by an ultimatum from the British promising support for the Egyptian government.

In 1949, after extensive mediation by the United Nations, armistice agreements were signed betwen Israel and most of the Arab states. Under the terms of these agreements, more territory was given to Israel than it had received in the original partition plan. Israel obtained the entire Negev, except for the Gaza Strip, which remained under Egyptian control, and a demilitarized zone under the control of the UN. Jerusalem was divided between Israel and Transjordan, which became known as Jordan. As for the Arab state created by the partition plan of 1947, it simply never materialized. Its territory was taken by Israel, Egypt, and Jordan. (See map, p. 22.)

[21]

Palestine
1922–1949

SYRIA

MEDITERRANEAN   SEA

LEBANON

● Beirut

● Damascus

FRENCH MANDATE

Lake Tiberias

Haifa ●

PALESTINE

Jordan R.

Tel Aviv ● ● Acre
Jaffa ●
    ● Deir Yassin
Jerusalem ●

Gaza Strip

Dead Sea

TRANSJORDAN

Suez Canal

Negev

BRITISH MANDATE

● Cairo

EGYPT

● Eilat

Sinai

Gulf of Aqaba

Sharm
el-Sheikh ●

Straits of Tiran

RED   SEA

French Mandate

British Mandate

Israel's borders set by
UN Partition Plan 1948

Proposed Arab state,
UN Partition Plan, 1948

Israel's borders
after 1948–49 war

THE PLIGHT OF THE PALESTINIAN ARABS

By the end of the 1948 war, hundreds of thousands of Arabs had fled their homes in Palestine. Unlike their Jewish neighbors, the Arabs were not organized to establish a state in Palestine. Some began to leave after the partition resolution was passed in November 1947. The acts of violence committed by both sides during the civil war also frightened many Arabs into leaving. On April 9, 1948, for example, the Irgun and another radical Israeli group, called the Stern Gang, captured the Arab town of Deir Yassin and murdered two hundred and fifty unarmed civilians, including women and children.

After war broke out in May, the flight of the Arabs increased. Many were forced to leave their homes by the Israeli army. The Israelis were fearful that the Palestinians might assist the invading Arabs. Israeli leaders also wanted to create a more homogeneous state consisting mainly of Jews. During the war many Arab towns were destroyed, and their land was later given to Jewish immigrants.

The majority of the Palestinians fled to Jordan; the rest went to Egypt, Lebanon, Syria, and other Arab states. Most could be found congregating in overcrowded refugee camps, mainly in Jordan and along the Gaza Strip. Eventually the camps were taken over by the UN, but funds to run them were inadequate, and the refugees lived a threadbare existence.

These Palestinians beame the outcasts of the Middle East. The Israelis would not allow them to return home, and there was little the Arab states could do for them. In Jordan, for example, the refugees were permitted to become citizens, but the government could provide few jobs for them because they were unskilled fellahin. The refugees faced a similar situation along the Gaza Strip, Lebanon, and Syria, where they found little land or other resources available. Many refugees also seemed reluc-

[23]

tant to begin new lives or find jobs in UN-sponsored work programs. Such a step seemed to foreclose the possibility that they would ever go home, or that Israel would ever compensate them for their lost land.

As the years went by, thousands of Palestinians remained in the refugee camps. When the refugees looked across the border into Israel, they longed to return home and felt angry and frustrated over their plight. For the Jews, 1948 marked the end of the Diaspora. For the Palestinian Arabs, a diaspora had just begun. They called it, appropriately, the Castastrophe.

3

Crisis at Suez

Although 1949 spelled an end to open warfare between the armies of Israel and the Arab states, there would be no lasting peace. The apparent stumbling block was the problem of the Palestinian refugees. The refugees themselves kept this issue alive and refused to let the Arab states forget them. When King Abdullah of Jordan tried to negotiate a peace treaty with Israel, he was assassinated on July 20, 1951, by a Palestinian. The fate of Abdullah served as a warning to any other Arab leader who might underestimate the importance of the Palestinians. Yet this wasn't the only issue that prevented the Arab heads of state from concluding peace with Israel. They felt humiliated by the results of the 1948 war and wanted the opportunity to avenge themselves through a crushing defeat of Israel. Only another conflict would provide that opportunity.

THE POSITION OF ISRAEL
Israel's military victories in 1948 still left it in a very precarious position. The new nation faced enemies on all sides who had left open the possibility of renewed conflict. Israel's borders with the Arab states stretched for

[25]

approximately 450 miles (600 km), an extensive line to defend. At some points the distance from the border to the Mediterranean Sea measured only a few miles. This meant that a rapid strike by the Arabs could easily cut the state of Israel in half.

Israeli leaders believed that in order to guard against the possibility of Arab invasion they had to maintain a constant state of military preparedness. But a large standing army would place far too great a strain on the Israeli economy. So Israeli leaders, headed by Prime Minister Ben-Gurion and military Chief of Staff Yigal Yadin, created a system of reserves. Under this system most men and women were required to serve in the armed forces. They were trained for duty and continued to be prepared for war, even though they did not remain on active service. In the event of a conflict, these reserves could be mobilized in a few days, forming a highly trained military force to supplement Israel's small standing army.

While the reserve system solved some problems, it was not a perfect solution. For instance, Israel could not allow itself to be surprised by an overwhelming Arab attack that might overrun the country before the reserves could be mobilized. To avoid this situation, Israeli leaders believed that they had to deliver the first attack if they suspected the Arabs were preparing for war. As a result, the so-called preemptive strike, designed to quickly knock out Arab resistance, became part of Israeli military planning. The preemptive strike also fit perfectly with another Israeli policy: to fight only short wars. Quite simply, Israel lacked the economic resources and the population for a long conflict.

As Israel prepared for the possibility of war, it continued to explore the prospects for peace with the Arabs. As a gesture of goodwill, a small number of Palestinians were permitted to return. But Israel insisted that the rest must find new homes in the Arab states. Meanwhile

Israeli leaders issued strong warnings against any attempt by the Arabs to increase their military power.

Israeli leaders generally believed there was little chance of improving relations with the Arab states in view of their current policies. The Arabs had refused to establish diplomatic relations with Israel and pressured third world countries not to grant it recognition. They had also closed their borders to Israeli citizens. In addition the Arabs had established an economic boycott against Israel. Egypt restricted the passage of goods bound for Israel through the Suez Canal and the Gulf of Aqaba. Thus, Israeli plans to turn Eilat into a prosperous seaport were destroyed. Clearly, the Arabs seemed intent on bringing an end to Israel's short existence.

Along the Arab-Israeli borders, conflicts erupted. In violation of the 1949 truce agreements, Israel established a military outpost in the demilitarized zone on its border with Egypt. This was aimed at defending Israel against Palestinian refugees in the Gaza Strip. Some of these refugees had been crossing from the Strip into Israel and creating incidents.

Conflicts also occurred on the Jordanian border. The armistice agreements had left some villages divided in half between Israel and Jordan. Palestinians who had been separated from their lands tried to cross into Israel and retake them from Jewish farmers. At first, there were only a few incidents. But the level of violence gradually increased until Arabs and Jews were mounting raids against each other.

In the north there were bloody disputes between Israel and Syria over Lake Tiberias. Both sides hurled claims and counterclaims at each other over their rights to use the lake for fishing and water resources.

A NEW REGIME IN EGYPT

In July 1952, the corrupt government of King Farouk of Egypt was overthrown by a military coup. This development would have a profound effect on Israel and upon the rest of the Middle East.

The leader of the coup was a young lieutenant-colonel named Gamal Abdel Nasser. Colonel Nasser had fought for Egypt during the 1948 war against Israel, and, like many Egyptians, he felt humiliated by the defeat. One of those who shared Nasser's feelings was Anwar el-Sadat who participated in the overthrow of the Farouk government. After the takeover, Sadat announced over Radio Cairo:

> *Egypt has lived through one of the darkest periods of its history. The army has been tainted by agents of dissolution. This was one of the causes of our defeat in Palestine. . . . This is why we have carried out a purge. The army is now in the hands of men in whose ability, integrity, and patriotism you can have complete confidence.*

In spite of Nasser's experiences in the '48 war, it appeared for a time that relations between Egypt and Israel might improve. Both countries, for example, were opposed to British influence in the Middle East. But after some initial contacts between Cairo and Jerusalem, nothing else happened. And relations between the two countries worsened.

By this time, Nasser's attention had turned to the Suez Canal. French engineers had built the canal during the nineteenth century to link together the Mediterranean with the Red Sea. Opened in 1869, the waterway was run by a joint stock company, with France owning a controlling share and the Egyptian khedive, or ruler, owning the rest. A few years later the khedive ran into severe financial problems and needed to raise money. So he sold his shares to the British, who saw the canal as a vital link to their empire in the Far East. To protect their interests and quell unrest, the British invaded Egypt in 1882, where they remained to rule the country as part of their far-flung empire. Although Egypt was eventually granted almost complete independence in the 1920s, Britain still retained some of its power and never gave up the right to keep a military force on the Suez Canal to defend that vital waterway.

As a zealous nationalist, it was important to Nasser to remove this military force as the last vestige of British imperialism. The British, at this time, were also anxious to avoid a conflict with the new Egyptian government and retain whatever influence they could in the Arab world. Consequently, in 1954 Britain agreed to remove its troops from the canal over the next twenty months.

The British decision was a great victory for Nasser, but it caused dismay in Israel. Although Israeli leaders held little affection for Great Britain, they regarded the British military presence as a protective buffer between Egypt and the Israeli frontier. With the departure of the British, that buffer would be gone. Egypt would also come into possession of modern British airfields and other military facilities on the canal. These might be used to launch an assault against Israel.

So ominous did the situation appear to some members of the Israeli government that they concocted a foolish scheme to prevent the British from leaving. Israeli saboteurs were ordered to destroy British and American property in Egypt and make it look as if Egyptians had committed these acts of sabotage. When the saboteurs were exposed and placed on trial in Cairo, relations between Egypt and Israel were damaged even further.

Meanwhile, Palestinian guerrillas continued infiltrating Israel and launching their terrorist attacks, killing unarmed civilians, including many children. In 1953, Moshe Dayan was appointed chief of staff of Israel's army, called the Israeli Defense Force (IDF). Dayan recalled in his autobiography that he found the army had

[29]

allowed its standards to decline during the years of relative peace since 1948 and it was often ineffective in dealing with terrorists. Dayan promptly began trying to raise standards. He also stepped up Israeli reprisal raids against Arab guerrilla bases, primarily in Jordan. The IDF, Dayan wrote, became more effective in dealing with the guerrillas, and the raids gave the soldiers valuable combat experience.

On February 28, 1955, Israel launched a different kind of raid. It was directed not at Arab guerrilla bases but at Egyptian army headquarters in the Gaza Strip. Thirty-eight Egyptians were killed and others lay wounded. David Ben-Gurion was quoted as saying that the raid had been designed "to teach Egypt a lesson." Yet historians disagree over whether Israel had any real provocation for launching such a raid against Egypt. According to historian Howard M. Sachar in his book *Egypt and Israel,* Nasser had already begun training the *fedayeen* (Palestinian terrorists) in Gaza and sending them against Israel. It was part of his effort to assert Egyptian leadership in the Arab world. But other historians say that Nasser only began sending in the fedayeen after the Israeli raid. Following the raid, Nasser himself stated: "This disaster was the warning bell. We at once started to examine the significance of peace and the balance of power in the area."

THE ROAD TO WAR
After the events of February 28, Nasser began to strengthen Egypt's military machine. This required modern weapons. Nasser tried to buy arms from the West, but when this proved unsuccessful, he obtained them from the Soviet bloc. The arms shipments, which started arriving in the fall of 1955, included jet fighters, bombers, tanks, and artillery.

In his autobiography, Dayan wrote that these shipments "tipped the arms balance drastically against

Israel." Dayan believed that the arms were designed to be used in an attack on Israel, which might begin any time in the near future. Consequently, he advised Ben-Gurion to consider launching preemptive strikes aimed at taking control of the Gaza Strip and capturing Sharm el-Sheikh, which commanded the Straits of Tiran at the entrance to the Gulf of Aqaba. The Egyptians had placed artillery in Sharm el-Sheikh to guard the straits and have control over which ships reached Israel.

At the same time, Israel looked around for its own arms supplier in order to combat the Egyptian military build-up. Britain, of course, was out of the question. The United States was trying to improve its relations with the Arab countries, hoping to gain influence with them and prevent another war in the Middle East, so Washington refused to sell Israel any arms. But in France, Israel finally found a willing supplier.

French leaders had been waiting for an opportunity to retaliate against Nasser for his involvement in the French colony of Algeria, in North Africa. Algeria had been under French control since the nineteenth century, but recently the Muslims, who constituted a majority of the population, had been pressing Paris for more political power leading eventually to independence. When the French resisted, Muslim groups attacked government offices and carried their revolt to many parts of the country. In Cairo, Nasser promised support to the Muslim rebels, and at a meeting of the Third World nations in 1955 he called for an independent Algeria. The French were outraged. In order to strike at Nasser, and strengthen their influence in the Middle East, they agreed to sell jets to Israel.

At the same time guerrilla warfare in the region was intensifying. Nasser continued his policy of launching fedayeen attacks against Israeli villages. And, seeking revenge, Israel sent its own commandos into the Gaza Strip. In September 1955, Nasser retaliated by tightening his control on the Straits of Tiran. More raids followed on both sides. The Egyptians struck an Israeli kibbutz, and Israel bombed a marketplace in Gaza. Nor was there peace along the other borders. Conflicts broke out between Syria and Israel over Lake Tiberias. Attacks and counterattacks also occurred with regularity between Israel and Jordan.

SUEZ AGAIN

Once again the focus of events in the Middle East shifted to the Suez Canal. In July 1956, after Britain had withdrawn its troops from Suez, Nasser made the following announcement:

> *Today we are not repeating the past. The Suez Canal Company became a state within a state, one which humiliated ministers and ministries and which humiliated everyone. The canal is an Egyptian canal. . . . Britain forcibly took away from us our right in it. . . .*
>
> *We shall never repeat the past, but we shall eliminate the past. We shall eliminate the past by regaining our rights to the Suez Canal.*
>
> *Therefore I have signed today and the government has approved the following: A resolution . . . for the nationalization of the Suez Canal.*

Nasser's sudden decision to take over the canal had not occurred without good reason, at least in his mind. It had been meant as a retaliation for actions taken earlier by Britain and the United States. Both countries had offered to help finance a high dam at Aswan on the Nile River. This was an important project to Nasser because the dam would improve the Egyptian economy by providing hydroelectric power and increased water supplies for irrigation. Then Britain and the United States withdrew their offer. They believed that Nasser had grown too independent in his foreign policies and that his relations with the Communist bloc had become much too close. Nasser's prestige and his economic program had been damaged, so he decided to strike where he could do the most harm—the canal. It was a vital link in the oil lifeline of Britain as well as France.

Nasser's action made him a hero in Egypt and in many parts of the Arab world. But he had taken a tremendous risk, for Britain and France might try to regain control of the canal by resorting to force. In his autobiography, Anwar Sadat recalls telling Nasser:

If you had consulted me, I would have told you to be more careful. This step means war, and we're not ready for it. The weapons we have, we've only just received from the Soviet Union . . . and we're not adequately trained to use the new weapons. But now that this decision has already been taken, of course, we should all support you. And I shall be the first to do so.

In London and Paris, planning started almost immediately for military action to regain the canal. Before summer's end, France had also involved a third partner, Israel, which had signaled its willingness to help. Allied with France and Britain, Israel hoped that in a short war against Egypt it could capture Sharm el-Sheikh and clear the Gaza Strip of fedayeen.

Exploratory talks took place between French and Israeli representatives. In late September Israel sent a delegation to Paris made up of high-level officials, including Chief of Staff Moshe Dayan, Foreign Minister Golda Meir, and Director-General of the Defense Ministry Shimon Peres. In their first meeting with French Foreign Minister Christian Pineau, they were told that France was eager for a joint operation with Israel against Egypt. However, Pineau was doubtful that the operation would be joined by Great Britain. While British Prime Minister Anthony Eden supported a military venture, he was opposed by other members of the British government. The Israelis responded by saying that they were prepared to cooperate with France. However, they opposed a French suggestion that Israel strike first and allow itself to be branded the aggressor. Further, they believed that no military campaign should be initiated until Britain had decided what to do.

Talks continued between Israel and France for some weeks without reaching any final agreement. During that time, Israel received additional shipments of French weapons to be used should an attack on Suez occur.

Finally, in late October another round of talks began at Sèvres, outside Paris. Discussions centered around the following proposal. A war against Egypt would begin with Israel advancing through the Sinai Desert toward Suez. Britain and France would then issue an ultimatum calling on Egypt and Israel to end hostilities and withdraw from the canal. The Egyptians were expected to ignore the ultimatum. French and British aircraft would then strike Egyptian airfields and demolish the planes which Egypt had received in the Soviet arms deal. During all the preliminary discussions with France, the Israelis had worried that Egypt might use these planes to destroy their army in the Sinai or to bomb population centers inside Israel. Finally, France and Britain would invade Egypt, retake the canal, and remove Nasser from power.

This plan satisfied the two Western powers because it allowed them to accomplish their goals while giving them a pretext to invade without seeming to be the aggressors. However, Ben-Gurion—who had accompanied the Israeli negotiating team this time—was adamantly opposed to having Israel strike first. As a compromise, Dayan suggested that Israel should drop a para-troop unit into the Sinai behind the Egyptian border. This could be seen as a reprisal attack for fedayeen raids instead of an Israeli first strike. Nevertheless, the para-troop force would be large enough to give Britain and France the pretext for issuing the ultimatum. Dayan's compromise was accepted and the date of the Israeli attack was set.

WAR AT SUEZ

On October 29, in accordance with the agreement at Sèvres, the Suez War began. Following the orders of Chief of Staff Moshe Dayan, Israeli paratroopers landed near the Mitla Pass, which cuts through the mountains of the western Sinai. The pass is located approximately 30 miles (48 km) east of the Suez Canal. On the same day other Israeli units crossed the frontier and began marching through Sinai to link up with the paratroopers at the pass.

At first the Egyptians believed that the paratroop drop was nothing more than a raid. But as more troops streamed over the border, the Egyptian high command realized a larger attack was under way. Troops were ordered into the Sinai to reinforce Egyptian units already stationed there. Meanwhile Egyptian forces contested the Israeli advance through the Mitla Pass. The battle lasted over two hours, and the Egyptians retreated only after putting up a stiff fight.

According to plan, France and Britain issued their ultimatum on October 30. It gave Egypt and Israel twelve hours to withdraw 10 miles (16 km) from the canal. Nasser rejected the ultimatum because it would have meant giving up some Egyptian territory while allowing Israel to remain on Egyptian soil. When the deadline passed, Britain and France were supposed to begin bombing Egyptian airfields. But the attack didn't come due to last-minute problems that British and French military planners hadn't anticipated. Only in the

[35]

Sinai did heavy fighting continue to rage as Dayan's troops kept pushing back the Egyptian forces.

Finally the Anglo-French bombing attacks began on the airfields near Suez. Nasser called his troops out of the Sinai to prevent them from being trapped between invading French and British forces from the west and Israeli units attacking from the east. As the Egyptian army retreated, the Israelis continued their advance toward Suez. Meanwhile Dayan's forces moved into Gaza and began destroying the fedayeen. In the south, Israeli units marched toward Sharm el-Sheikh, which fell in early November. (See map, p. 22.) While Israel was securing its objectives, Britain and France landed at the Suez Canal.

As the allies were scoring military triumphs in the Middle east, strenuous diplomatic efforts had been under way in other quarters to bring the war to an immediate end. From the start, the United States had opposed the French-British-Israeli operation. Now, under pressure from the U.S. and threats of possible intervention in the war by the Soviet Union, Britain and France agreed to a cease-fire before they had taken complete control of the Suez Canal.

At home, meanwhile, Eden was being sharply criticized for starting the war. Nasser had retaliated against Britain and France by sinking ships in the canal and cutting the oil supply line. The United Nations was also calling for the withdrawal of foreign troops from Egyptian soil. Finally, in December, Britain and France bowed to world opinion and began evacuating their forces. All of them had gone before the end of the month.

In December, Israel was also forced to begin withdrawing its troops, after threats by the United States to cut off foreign aid. However, Ben-Gurion refused to leave the Gaza Strip or Sharm el-Sheikh, even in the face of U.S. pressure and repeated resolutions by the United Nations General Assembly. Speaking on the subject of Gaza before the Assembly, Golda Meir stated:

[36]

It is inconceivable that the nightmare of the previous eight years should be reestablished in Gaza with international sanction. Shall Egypt be allowed once more to organize murder and sabotage in this Strip?

But the pressure applied on the Israeli government remained unrelenting. Finally a compromise was worked out. The Israelis agreed to withdraw from Gaza and Sharm el-Sheikh, where they were to be replaced by a United Nations Emergency Force (UNEF). In addition the United States agreed to join with other powers to secure Israel's access to the Gulf of Aqaba.

It was not a perfect solution, at least as far as the Israeli leaders were concerned. Nevertheless, the Gulf of Aqaba did remain open, and fedayeen raids from Gaza were almost completely stopped. As a result of the war, Israel's position in the Middle East had improved.

But, in fact, the Israelis may have lost almost as much as they gained. To many Arabs, Israel appeared to be little more than a tool of Western interests. And the Israeli victory made the Arab states even more eager to seek revenge and destroy the Jewish state. Surprisingly, the Suez War had greatly improved Nasser's position. Although his armies had been defeated and his country occupied, the Egyptian leader had achieved the withdrawal of the French, British, and Israeli forces. This was seen as a great moral victory in the Arab world, and Nasser's prestige rose to new heights.

4

Six Days
in June

Following the Suez crisis, Israel and its Arab neighbors
experienced almost a decade of relative peace. During
that period Israel enjoyed tremendous growth as thousands of Jewish immigrants streamed into the country
from Europe and North Africa. After surviving the 1948
war and winning a victory, even if it was short-lived, in
1957, Israel seemed like a secure place in which to live
and raise a family.

Many of the immigrants settled in the Negev Desert
where they set about transforming this barren region into
an economically productive area. Large communities
sprang up and became centers of commerce and industry. Modern shipping facilities were constructed at Eilat,
which was fast developing into a major seaport now that
the Straits of Tiran were open to Israeli vessels. Vast
acres of desert were also turned into fertile farmland that
bloomed with a variety of lush crops.

The miracle in the Negev would have been impossible without water for irrigation and industry. By 1964,
Israel had completed a huge project diverting water from
the Jordan River, which flowed along the Israeli border,

into the broad Negev region. The project had required many years of work and large financial outlays, and it had continuously run into strong opposition from the neighboring Arab countries. They saw it as an attempt to strengthen the state of Israel at the expense of Jordan, which would be losing part of its water supply. In 1960, the Arab League had denounced the project. Three years later Arab leaders again warned Israel against completing it. Both measures were initiated by Syria, whose regime was strongly opposed to the presence of a Jewish state. Israeli leaders, in turn, issued a stern warning that any attempt to stop the project would be met by force. Disregarding the Israeli threat, Syria and Lebanon did try to stop it. But they were driven off by Israeli planes and artillery.

Along the Syrian border, violence occurred with alarming regularity. Syrian troops on the Golan Heights repeatedly fired down on kibbutzim, leading to Israeli reprisal raids. Conflict also broke out on Lake Tiberias, where Syrian and Israeli gunboats engaged each other in a fierce battle. This brush-fire war acted as a constant irritant between Israel and Syria, keeping tensions high and creating a potentially dangerous situation that could eventually explode into another Middle East conflagration.

THE PALESTINIAN GUERRILLAS

A major source of friction between Israel and its neighbors were the Palestinian guerrillas, who operated from bases inside the Arab states. In 1964 the Palestine Liberation Organization (PLO) was established under the auspices of the Arab League. The PLO soon organized a small army of fedayeen, who began mounting attacks against Israel from across the border in Jordan.

Another, more radical, Palestinian group which had also started raiding Israeli settlements was al-Fatah. One of its founders was Yasir Arafat. Born and raised in

Jerusalem, Arafat had joined with other Palestinian Arabs to fight the Israelis in 1948. He later fled Israel, along with thousands of refugees, making his way to Gaza and eventually Cairo. Here Arafat attended Cairo University and studied engineering. After the Suez crisis, he left Cairo for Kuwait, where there were many opportunities for engineers in the burgeoning oil fields.

In Kuwait, Arafat and other Palestinian leaders established al-Fatah, which committed itself to regaining Palestine for the Arabs and destroying the state of Israel. Fatah believed that this goal could be achieved only by the Palestinians themselves, for it was convinced that the Arab states had abandoned the Palestinian cause. In Fatah's magazine *Our Palestine,* its leaders sought to inspire the Palestinians to rise up and make the world listen to their demands:

> *Sons of the Catastrophe, you cannot forget . . . the loss of land and honor. . . .*
>
> *Our destiny is being shaped, but our voice is not heard. . . . we tell you that our voice, the voice of the Palestinian people, will not be heard until the sons of Palestine stand together in one rank. . . . then you will find the world attentive to your merest whisper. . . . yes, just a whisper.*

Arafat traveled the Middle East hoping to solicit support for Fatah from Arab leaders. Most of them turned a deaf ear to him because they believed his organization was much too radical and might easily drag them into another war with Israel. But there was an exception, Syria, which favored a terrorist campaign against the Israeli state. Consequently, Fatah was permitted to establish guerrilla bases inside Syria from which to mount terrorist assaults on kibbutzim. But instead of launching raids across the Syrian border, the guerrillas chose to attack from Jordan, where the border was longer and less well defended.

In 1965 Fatah attacked some of Israel's water projects. This led Israeli Prime Minister Levi Eshkol to warn Jordan that it must keep the guerillas under control. When the raids continued, Israel launched reprisal attacks against Jordanian villages suspected of harboring the terrorists. Israeli planes were later sent into Syria where the guerrilla raids had originated.

In November 1966, Israel launched an unusually large attack against the Jordanian village of Samu, suspected of being a sanctuary for Palestinian terrorists. By the time the raid had ended, a number of unarmed Jordanian civilians lay dead or wounded. Israel's action provoked an outcry in many parts of the Arab world. Riots and demonstrations broke out among the Palestinians living in Jordan, who demanded that King Hussein supply arms to the villages along the border. Syria and Egypt called on Hussein to change his moderate position toward Israel and assume a much tougher stance. Meanwhile, the UN Security Council voted to censure Israel.

A serious conflict then erupted along the Syrian-Israeli border. On April 7, 1967, Syrian pilots, flying Russian MIG jets, engaged Israeli planes over Syrian territory. Six of the MIGs were shot down, and Syrian officials feared their capital at Damascus might be in jeopardy. At this point, they sent out an urgent appeal for help to Egypt, with whom Syria had signed a defensive military alliance. This proved to be the first in a series of steps that would ultimately lead only two months later to the third Arab-Israeli war.

THE POSITION OF EGYPT
The Syrian appeal found Egyptian President Nasser in a rather uncomfortable situation. For years he had cau-

tioned the other Arab states against another military conflict with Israel. He believed they were not strong enough to win such a war, even though his own country as well as Syria had been receiving large infusions of military aid from the Soviet Union. There were other reasons that Nasser wanted to avoid a conflict. The Egyptian economy was struggling, despite substantial assistance from the Communist bloc. In order to enhance its position in the Middle East, the Soviet Union had helped Egypt expand its industries and create thousands of new jobs. But a swollen bureaucracy and an unwieldy military establishment proved far too much for the Egyptian economy to support.

For the past four years the Egyptian military leaders had been preoccupied with a war in Yemen on the Arabian peninsula. In September 1962 a military coup had overthrown the royalist government there. Nasser extended diplomatic recognition to the new regime almost immediately, and when it called on him for military assistance to prevent the royalists from regaining control, he began sending in Egyptian troops. Saudi Arabia, meanwhile, started providing support to the other side. Yemen became the scene of a fierce civil war, which eventually tied up about seventy thousand of Nasser's finest soldiers. He would later call it appropriately "my Vietnam."

While the state of the Egyptian economy and the ruinous war in Yemen provided excellent reasons for Nasser to avoid a confrontation with Israel, strong pressure was building on him to act. Other Arab leaders were verbally attacking him because he had failed to retaliate for the repeated Israeli raids. They accused Nasser of being content to "hide" behind the UNEF forces in the Gaza Strip and Sharm el-Sheikh. Suddenly, Nasser's prestige and position of leadership in the Middle East seemed to be in jeopardy. Meanwhile, Syrian and Russian intelligence sources were passing on information to

[42]

the Egyptian president concerning large Israeli troop buildups in preparation for an invasion of Syria. Although the information was false and Nasser probably knew it, he may have thought that the Soviets would support him if he acted. Indeed, Nasser may have believed that they wanted him to act, and he felt obliged to do so.

In May 1967, Nasser placed his armed forces on alert and began moving military units into the Sinai. Then, to silence his critics in the Arab world, he called on UN Secretary-General U Thant to withdraw some of the UNEF troops from around the Gaza Strip and move them inside it. However, U Thant replied that he could not comply with Nasser's request. The entire force had to remain in position and do its job, U Thant said, or all of it must go. At this point, Nasser could not back down without losing face, so he called on the secretary-general to withdraw the entire military contingent. Its positions at Gaza and Sharm el-Sheikh were taken over by Egyptian armed forces.

Having reoccupied Sharm el-Sheikh, Nasser now made another decision. He closed the Straits of Tiran to Israeli shipping. The Israelis had fought for free passage through the Straits in 1957 and they regarded it as vital to their national survival. As Anwar Sadat stated in his autobiography, *In Search of Identity,* with "the Tiran Strait closed, war became a certainty."

Step by step, Nasser had moved along the road to another war. At first his objectives seemed to have been only limited ones: issuing a strong warning to Israel and recovering his lost prestige. But each time Nasser acted, the prospect of war became more certain. Somehow, he had forgotten all his warnings against another conflict and apparently convinced himself that the Arabs could win. Perhaps he was persuaded by the military power arrayed against Israel. In the north, Syria had mobilized its forces. On May 30, King Hussein signed an agree-

[43]

ment with Nasser to cooperate with the Egyptian forces in the event of war. A few days later, Iraq joined the alliance. Offers of military support also came from Morocco, Tunisia, and Saudi Arabia.

In the midst of the crisis Nasser boldly stated:

> *If Israel begins with any aggression against Egypt or Syria, the battle against Israel will be total and its object will be the destruction of Israel.*
>
> *We can do this. I could not have spoken like that five years ago or three years ago. . . . Today, eleven years after 1956, I say these words because I know what we have. . . . This is Arab power; this is the true rebirth of the Arab nation. . . .*

THE MOOD IN ISRAEL

Nasser's optimism about eventual victory resulted, in part, from Israel's rather weak response to the Arab military buildup. When Egyptian army units had first been directed into the Sinai, the government of Prime Minister Levi Eshkol did not view it with undue alarm. They believed Egypt was too weak to begin another war. Only after Nasser asked for the withdrawal of the UNEF troops did Eshkol order a mobilization of the Israeli reserves. But he still called on Egypt and Syria to join with Israel and bring about a peaceful end to the crisis:

> *I wish to repeat . . . especially to Egypt and Syria, that we do not contemplate any military action. . . . We have contemplated no intervention in their internal affairs. We ask only from these states the application of these same principles toward us as an act of reciprocity.*

Eshkol reacted to Nasser's next step—the closing of the Straits of Tiran—more forcefully. He branded it a "gross violation of international law" and "an act of aggression." Yet he still hoped that war could be avoided by diplomatic means. A short time later, Eshkol dispatched his foreign minister, Abba Eban, to Paris, London, and Washington to gain the support of the big powers and persuade them to intervene. Eban reminded Western leaders of their pledges after the 1956 Suez crisis to guarantee free access to the Straits of Tiran, and he called on them now to back up these pledges. In Paris, President Charles de Gaulle rejected Eban's appeal. Britain and the United States were initially more receptive. They discussed the possibility of organizing a joint international naval force to sail to the straits. But this force never materialized.

Although Israel continued to mobilize, the Eshkol government's apparently faint-hearted approach to war began to draw strong criticism from the Israeli people. Newspaper editorials expressed a lack of confidence in the prime minister's leadership, and they called on him to show greater firmness toward the Arabs. There were also expressions of dissatisfaction from important political leaders and some of Eshkol's cabinet ministers. Finally, under intense pressure from the members of his own government, Eshkol agreed to appoint Moshe Dayan as defense minister. The victor of the 1956 war was the one man in whom the Israeli people, now facing another conflict, had full confidence. In addition, Eshkol invited members of the opposition parties into his cabinet to form a government of national unity.

Eshkol had finally decided that another war was inevitable, and preparations for it now began in earnest. Dayan recounts in his autobiography that at a cabinet meeting on June 2 he recommended launching a "military strike without delay." His objectives were limited. Dayan proposed to crush the Egyptian forces in the

Sinai, while taking up a defensive position on all the other fronts. Over the next two days, he continued to urge a preemptive strike. This would give Israel the element of surprise and allow its planes to knock out part of the Egyptian air force, which was essential to victory in the Sinai. Delaying too long, Dayan cautioned, would only permit the Arabs to continue their buildup, making Israeli victory far more difficult.

Accordingly, a preemptive strike was set for June 5, 1967.

THE SIX DAY WAR

In the morning hours of June 5, squadrons of jet aircraft took off from airfields inside Israel and headed for Egypt. Nasser had decided to let Israel strike first so that he would not be branded the aggressor. In the first strike, the Egyptian president believed, he would lose about twenty percent of his aircraft—a loss he could sustain. Then he would launch his planes against Israel and avenge the defeat of 1956.

Soon the Israeli pilots had reached their destinations. Flying in low to escape radar detection, they struck Egyptian airfields in the Sinai, near the Suez Canal, and along the Nile River. Again and again the planes came in, hitting hundreds of aircraft parked on the runways and destroying the airfields. Israeli planes also struck radar installations and surface-to-air missile (SAM) sites. In a short time, the attack was over. Instead of losing twenty percent of his aircraft, Nasser's air power had been almost totally knocked out.

The other Arab countries were unaware of the magnitude of the Egyptian debacle. In fact, King Hussein was informed by the Egyptians that they had destroyed most of the Israeli air force and had gone on the offensive. Consequently, Hussein launched his own assault against Israel from the east. In response, the Israelis mounted another air strike aimed at Jordan. The result:

Hussein's small air force was totally destroyed. The same day Syria's air force also sustained heavy losses at the hands of Israeli jets.

Israel now had complete air superiority. It was an advantage that would be decisive. As the planes were attacking Egyptian airfields, Israeli armor and infantry moved against Egypt's fortified positions in the Sinai. A strong force advanced along the coast road in the northern Sinai and struck at El-Arish, which fell after a heavy air bombardment. Egyptian strongholds around Abu Agheila were also overrun and captured. The Israelis now continued their rapid march through the Sinai, as some units pushed further down the coast road toward the Suez Canal, and others drove the Egyptians toward the Gidi and Mitla passes through the mountains in the western part of the peninsula. Here the Israelis succeeded in getting behind the Egyptians and cutting off many of their troops. Following a battle at the passes, Israeli forces advanced toward the Gulf of Suez. In the south, meanwhile, the Egyptians evacuated Sharm el-Sheikh which was then occupied by Israeli forces.

On June 8, Egypt accepted a cease-fire which had been adopted in the UN Security Council. By this time, Israel controlled the entire Sinai and stood poised on the Suez Canal.

Israeli military achievements were not limited to the southern front. In the east, Jordanian troops had attacked the Jewish section of Jerusalem (the New City). With the assistance of a fierce aerial bombardment, Israeli armor and paratroopers counterattacked, driving the Jordanian army off the mountains overlooking Jerusalem. The IDF then entered the Old City, which had been part of Jordan, and captured the Arab defenders. The entire city of Jerusalem was now under Israeli control. But the Israelis did not stop here. In the north they captured the Jordanian villages of Ramalla and Nablus. They took Jericho in the east and advanced toward the Jordan River. To the south, Israeli units entered Bethlehem and Hebron, the town where Hebrew patriarchs were buried. As a result of the war with Jordan, Israel had taken complete possession of two areas which had formed part of the ancient kingdom of David—Judea and Samaria, also known as the West Bank.

Along the northern front, meanwhile, conditions had remained relatively quiet. After losing part of its air force, Syria had decided against an attack on Israel and assumed a defensive posture. Then on June 9, with Egypt and Jordan defeated, the IDF launched an assault on Syrian positions in the Golan Heights. A brutal battle followed as Israeli armor and infantry, along with strong air support, attempted to overrun the Syrian strongholds. Eventually, the Syrians were overwhelmed by a series of coordinated Israeli thrusts that penetrated the Golan in different locations. Syrian forces withdrew on June 10 and retreated to Damascus. A cease-fire followed that evening.

The Six Day War pointed out the vast military superiority of the Israeli forces over the Arabs. The Israeli soldiers had been well trained and boldly led in a series of lightning campaigns that had confounded their opponents. On the other side, the Arab soldiers suffered from a lack of education and training. Their leaders had proven totally inept, and they had made very little attempt to coordinate the Arab attacks in any kind of grand strategy. The result was total defeat. While Israeli dead numbered less than one thousand, Arab losses were many times that figure.

In terms of territorial gain, Israel had taken control of the Sinai, the Gaza Strip, East Jerusalem, the West Bank of the Jordan River (Judea and Samaria), and the Golan Heights. These acquisitions had vastly improved Israel's strategic position. No longer could Syrian gunners fire down on kibbutzim from the Golan Heights. The Jordanian bulge into the heart of Israel was gone

Israel and the Arab States

SYRIA

LEBANON

MEDITERRANEAN SEA

• Beirut

Latani R.

• Damascus

Golan Heights —

Lake Tiberias ◯

ISRAEL

West
Bank

Jordan R.

Tel Aviv •
Jerusalem •
Bethlehem •
Hebron •

• Amman

Jericho

*Dead
Sea*

Port Said •

Gaza Strip —

Suez
Canal

Beersheba •

Cairo •

▲ Gidi Pass

▲ Mitla Pass

JORDAN

EGYPT

Sinai

SAUDI ARABIA

Sharm
el-Sheikh

*Straits of
Tiran*

	Land gained in 1967 war
	Israeli positions after 1973 war
	Land returned to Egypt in peace treaty, 1980–1982

University School
Media Center

too. And in the south, Israeli forces sat along the Suez Canal. (See map, p. 49.)

The possibility that Israel would ever again confront the same situation it faced in 1948, when the new state was almost destroyed, seemed to have almost vanished. A larger territory meant more time to react in the event of another Arab attack. The Israeli army would be able to take up defensive positions away from Israel proper. And Israel could not so easily be cut in two by an Arab thrust aimed at its center. In fact, Israel now posed a much greater threat to the Arab states because its forces now lay much closer to Damascus, Amman, and Cairo.

While Israel celebrated its triumph, an atmosphere of gloom descended over the Arab states that had been engaged in the war. On June 10, President Nasser announced his resignation. However, an outpouring of public support from the Egyptian people, which had probably been engineered by Nasser himself, "persuaded" him to change his mind.

At the United Nations the Soviet Union was making strenuous efforts to secure passage of a resolution that would force Israel to withdraw from the conquered territories. But this resolution was strongly opposed by the United States and its allies. Eventually, after months of wrangling, the Security Council adopted a rather ambiguous measure known as Resolution 242. It called for:

I) withdrawal of Israeli armed forces from territories occupied in the recent conflict;

II) termination of all claims or states of belligerency and respect for and acknowledgement of the sovereignty, territorial integrity, and political independence of every state in the area and their right to live in peace within secure and recognized boundaries free from threats or acts of force. . . .

The resolution also included sections "guaranteeing free-dom of navigation through international waterways in the area" and "achieving a just settlement of the refugee problem. . . . "

Israel and the Arab states chose to put their own differing interpretations on the resolution. The Arabs believed it meant that Israel should withdraw from all the conquered territories. The Israelis pointed out that the word "all" had not been included in the resolution. Further, they stated that withdrawal could only occur as part of a comprehensive settlement in which the Arab states recognized Israel's right to live in peace and within secure boundaries. Israel and the Arab states would constantly cite Resolution 242 as the only basis for a firm and lasting peace between them. But, since they couldn't agree on the meaning of the resolution, they could hardly negotiate the terms of peace.

5

Yom Kippur, 1973

In the Middle East, conflict had seemingly become the natural state of affairs, so there was little reason to expect that the situation would change suddenly after the 1967 war. In fact, violence broke out along the Suez Canal shortly after the cease-fire went into effect. Egyptian commandos struck at Israeli military installations. Artillery duels erupted across the canal, after the Arabs claimed that Israel had begun shelling civilian population centers in the area. Finally, Israel began sending its air force against targets deep inside Egyptian territory. In October a serious incident occurred when an Egyptian vessel carrying Soviet missiles sank the Israeli destroyer *Eilat* off the coast of Sinai. Israel took its revenge by destroying Egyptian oil facilities at Suez.

As the conflict continued, Nasser's position along the canal grew steadily stronger. Shortly after the Six Day War ended, the Soviets began shipping new military supplies to Egypt and Syria to replace all the hardware they had lost on the battlefield. Egypt received tanks, planes, and SAM batteries, as well as ten thousand Communist bloc advisors.

In return, Nasser agreed to provide the USSR with naval facilities at Alexandria and Port Said. Israel, meantime, began to build up its own forces and acquired Phantom jets from the United States.

In April 1969, Nasser announced that the cease-fire following the '67 war had ended. The War of Attrition, in which each side tried to wear down the other, now formally began, although it had actually been underway for some time. Nasser's artillery shelled the newly constructed Israeli fortified position on the canal known as the Bar-Lev line, after Israeli Chief of Staff Chaim Bar-Lev. Israeli Defense Minister Dayan retaliated by bombarding the Egyptian canal cities. Dayan also sent his planes and commandos on extensive raids against surface-to-air missile (SAM) sites, radar installations, and military bases. The Israelis struck many locations in Egypt, prompting Nasser to send out an urgent appeal to Moscow for more reinforcements.

The Soviet Union strengthened Nasser's defenses with new SAM missiles and more advisors. In addition, the Soviets agreed to fly reconnaissance missions for Egypt and to man the SAM installations. Thus, the Soviets and the Israelis found themselves confronting each other directly, and conflict between them could occur at almost any moment. Dayan tried to avoid this situation by ending his raids against the SAM batteries. But when these were gradually moved closer to the canal, he reversed his decision and ordered his planes to destroy them. At the same time, Russian and Israeli pilots began encountering each other during their missions. And finally on July 30, 1970, Israeli planes shot down some Russian MIGs.

This type of incident might have blown up into a larger conflict, but in August, Israel and Egypt agreed to an American cease-fire proposal. Surprisingly it remained in effect for three years.

[53]

THE PALESTINIANS

As a result of its victory in 1967, Israel gained control over one million Arabs living on the West Bank and in the Gaza Strip (a narrow piece of territory along the Mediterranean which had been controlled by Egypt). Administering these territories became the direct responsibility of Moshe Dayan, the defense minister. Dayan kept the Israeli military presence to a minimum and allowed local Arab officials to continue running many day-to-day affairs. Further, Dayan instituted the so-called open bridges policy, allowing Jews to travel to the conquered territories and Arabs there to travel into Israel or across the Jordan. As a result, the residents of the West Bank and Gaza did not feel cut off from the rest of the Arab world. "Open bridges" had important economic effects too. Many Palestinian refugees, who had been unemployed since 1948, could now go to Israel, where they found jobs. A brisk trade was also carried on between Arabs on the West Bank and in the kingdom of Jordan, which proved beneficial to people on both sides of the river.

Nevertheless, the Israeli occupation proved to be oppressive for the Arabs. As Edward Said points out in his book *The Question of Palestine,* the Arabs on the West Bank lost their Jordanian citizenship and were not given the rights of citizenship in Israel. In addition, any Arabs whom the Israelis thought to be undesirable were immediately deported. And Arabs suspected of harboring Palestinian terrorists were punished by having their homes destroyed. This was part of Dayan's attempt to defeat the Palestinian commandos who were busy infiltrating the occupied territories. The commandos often resorted to terrorist bombings in an effort to keep local Arabs from working in Israel. Dayan retaliated by capturing or killing hundreds of members of al-Fatah and other terrorist groups.

In March 1968, the Israelis crossed the Jordan River and attacked the town of Karameh, thought to be a Palestinian commando base. With the support of Jordanian troops, Fatah put up an unusually stiff fight, which cost the Israelis heavily. Dayan reported that his units lost about twenty-nine killed and ninety wounded in capturing the town. Such heavy losses were a first for the Israelis in a raid against the commandos. Fatah leaders claimed that the Battle of Karameh was proof they could defend themselves against Israeli forces.

Following the battle, the prestige of Fatah grew enormously. Their membership increased, and they began mounting more raids against Israel. In Jordan the commandos had become so powerful that they were regarded as a "state within a state" which King Hussein seemed unable or unwilling to control. Yasir Arafat then expanded Fatah's operation to Lebanon, securing permission from the Lebanese government to establish a small group of commandos there in 1968. Gradually they took control of the Palestinian refugee camps in Lebanon, using them as training grounds and as bases for raids. The Israelis, in turn, launched repeated attacks into Lebanon and Jordan designed to root out the guerrillas and force these two Arab governments to restrict the terrorists' operations.

Inside Jordan, tension between the commandos and King Hussein was mounting. In September 1970, the Popular Front for the Liberation of Palestine (PFLP), an extremely radical Palestinian group, hijacked four commercial airliners and forced three of them to land on a secluded airfield inside Jordan. The hijackers announced that they would hold the passengers pending the release of PFLP terrorists who had been imprisoned in Europe. When the European governments holding the terrorists agreed to the hijackers' demands, all the passengers were freed.

Shortly after this incident, which had demonstrated the ineffectiveness of his regime, King Hussein decided to strike at the Palestinian guerrillas. Hussein directed his army against the guerrilla camps located around the capital, Amman, and in other parts of the country. By the middle of 1971 he had rounded up or killed thousands of guerrillas and crushed their power inside Jordan. Arafat and the Palestinians then moved their base of operations to Lebanon.

A NEW EGYPTIAN LEADER

In September 1970, while trying to bring about a peace agreement between King Hussein and Yasir Arafat, President Nasser died of a massive heart attack. Nasser's handpicked successor, Anwar el-Sadat, became the new Egyptian president. A change of leadership in Cairo seemed to open the faint possibility of negotiations between Egypt and Israel. Proposals involving the withdrawal of Israeli troops were forthcoming from both sides, but there was no agreement. Finally, in apparent frustration, Sadat announced that 1971 would be the "year of decision." Either the stalemate with Israel would be broken by peaceful means or he would resort to war.

To back up his pledge, Sadat repeatedly demanded more arms from Moscow. But the Soviets refused to give him the hardware he requested, so the Egyptian president felt unable to challenge Israel in another war. When 1971 drew to a close, Israeli forces remained along the Suez Canal, there was no prospect of peace, and Anwar Sadat looked to all the world like a fool.

Meanwhile, Sadat had been growing tired of the Soviet presence inside his country. He was also angered by the attitudes of the Soviet technicians who tended to treat the Egyptians as inferiors. After submitting additional requests for military assistance and receiving the same negative response from Moscow, Sadat finally ordered the Soviet advisors to leave Egypt in July 1972. In his autobiography, Sadat explains this decision:

[56]

One of the reasons behind my decision was the Soviet attitude to me; but another important reason was that within the strategy I had laid down, no war could be fought while Soviet experts worked in Egypt. . . . A further reason for the expulsion of the Soviet experts was that the Soviet Union had begun to feel that it enjoyed a privileged position in Egypt. . . . I wanted to put the Soviet Union in its place.

It may seem surprising that the Egyptian president had decided on another war with Israel. But Sadat believed that he had to take this risk regardless of his military strength. He was firmly convinced that any victory, no matter how small, was the only way to regain his country's prestige and bring Israel to the bargaining table, where he might regain the Sinai. The expulsion of the Soviet advisors gave Sadat the flexibility he needed to begin preparing for a war now without any restraint from Moscow.

Sadat envisioned a very limited type of conflict in keeping with the limitations on his armed forces. He proposed to launch an attack across the Suez Canal, seize a small strip of territory occupied by the Israelis, and hold it. Then he would wait for the Israeli armies to exhaust themselves as they sought to dislodge him from his defensive position. Sadat's strategy had the added advantrage of neutralizing the Israeli air force. For if his army remained close to the canal, it could be protected by the SAM batteries, which would shoot down the Israeli jets.

The Egyptian president did not propose to take on the Israelis by himself. He enlisted the support of Syria's President Hafez al-Assad, whose task would be to dislodge Israeli forces from the Golan Heights. Sadat also received a promise of limited support from Jordan.

When he expelled the Soviet advisors, Sadat had

wisely refrained from cutting all his ties with Moscow. He still permitted the Russian Mediterranean fleet to use Egyptian naval facilities under the terms of the agreement signed by Nasser. At the end of 1972, Sadat informed the Soviet Union that he had decided to extend that agreement. Following this decision, the Soviets began to fill Sadat's request for renewed shipments of SAM missiles.

Throughout 1973, Sadat strengthened his position for the coming war. This time he did not plan to wait for the Israelis to strike first: Sadat wanted the element of surprise. By early summer he had selected the date for the surprise attack—October 6, 1973. It was Yom Kippur, the Day of Atonement, the most important of Jewish holy days. On this day, the Israelis would be occupied with prayer and fasting.

ISRAEL MISREADS THE SIGNS

During September and early October, as Egyptian and Syrian troops completed the final buildup for battle, their movements were watched by Israeli intelligence. In fact, the intelligence service had been monitoring the Arab preparations all along. But it failed to interpret these maneuvers correctly, because intelligence was convinced that Egypt and Syria were not strong enough even to contemplate starting another war.

Without absolute assurance from the intelligence service that war was coming, the Israeli government hesitated to mobilize the reserves. Earlier that year, when it looked as if Syria might enter Lebanon, Prime Minister Golda Meir had ordered a full mobilization, costing the government millions of dollars. It had been a false alarm, and Israel did not wish to repeat this mistake. Therefore, it was not until October 5, when all the available intelligence now pointed to an imminent attack, that Mrs. Meir called for a partial mobilization. Next morning, Yom Kippur, the intelligence service was finally convinced that the war would begin at six P.M. that day. Mrs. Meir then ordered a full mobilization. Unfortunately, she had waited too long. The Arab attack commenced at two P.M.; it would be days before the Israeli reserves could be fully mobilized.

Under the protection of an enormous artillery barrage, Egyptian troops began to cross the Suez Canal and establish themselves on the eastern side. Soon the Egyptians had overrun the lightly held Bar-Lev Line that served as an Israeli advance position. Caught off-guard, the Israelis tried to organize their tanks and launch a strong counterattack to regain the line, but they were repulsed, suffering heavy losses. By the 7th of October, the Egyptian Second and Third Armies had established their positions along the canal where they waited for the Israelis to renew their attack and exhaust themselves, as Sadat had planned. On the 8th, a second Israeli assault did come. Since Jerusalem had not yet been able to fully mobilize the reserves and send them to the front, the assault proved far too weak to dislodge the Egyptians. Once again, Israeli casualties were staggering.

Along the northern front Syrian troops attacked Israeli positions on the Golan Heights. At first, it appeared that the Israelis might hold out. But by October 7, the Syrians had overcome Jewish resistance in one sector and began heading southward. Defense Minister Dayan immediately ordered his air force to concentrate against the Syrian advance, which now posed a serious threat to the heart of Israel. With adequate air support, Israeli armor and infantry finally slowed the Syrian attack. Israel now had time to rush in reserve units and strengthen its lines. With the forces in the north reinforced, Dayan launched a fierce counterattack that proved more than a match for the Syrians. Eventually, they were driven off the Golan Heights; and by October 10, the Israelis had reoccupied almost all the territory they had held before the war.

But Israeli casualties were far heavier than they had been in 1967. Many lives, scores of planes, and hundreds of tanks had already been lost along the northern and southern fronts. Israel could not easily withstand these losses and still hope to defeat the Arab forces, whose numbers were vastly superior.

At this point, the Israelis sent out an urgent appeal to the United States for military supplies. Washington might have preferred that the Israelis agree to a cease-fire, since a relative stalemate now existed on the Syrian and the Egyptian fronts. At the same time, the Soviets were putting pressure on Sadat to bring an end to the conflict. But the Egyptian president refused, because he believed the Israeli army had not been sufficiently damaged. Since the Soviet Union could not allow Egypt and Syria to be defeated, it began to resupply them with enormous quantities of arms and ammunition so they could hold out through a longer war. On the other side, Washington now started to resupply Israel to prevent its forces from being overwhelmed.

Along the northern front Israel renewed its offensive against the Syrians in an attempt to destroy their army and take them out of the war. This task proved much harder than the Israelis had anticipated. Supported by troops from Iraq and Jordan, the Syrians put up a spirited defense. After a few days of combat, the Israelis succeeded in advancing toward Damascus, but the Syrians and their allies continued to resist stubbornly. The military situation in the north became a standoff.

In order to relieve the pressure on themselves, the Syrians had earlier asked Sadat to launch a major new attack in the Sinai. The assault began on October 14, but this time the Israelis had been reinforced by their reserves, and they succeeded in smashing the Egyptian onslaught. The Israeli army then went over to the offensive. In a daring maneuver, they sent some of their units between the two Egyptian armies positioned along the

[60]

east bank of the canal and crossed it. Once on the other side, these units began fanning out north and south, putting the Egyptians into a trap between Israeli forces on either side of the canal. (See map, p. 49.) At first, Sadat was unaware of what had happened. But as the full impact of the Israeli breakthrough became evident, he called on the Soviets to try to bring about a cease-fire.

At the suggestion of the Russians, Secretary of State Henry Kissinger went to Moscow, where an agreement was finally worked out. It called for a cease-fire and eventual face-to-face negotiations between Israel and the Arab states. This had long been an important aim of the Israeli government. The Soviet-American agreement received the backing of Jerusalem, Cairo and Amman on October 22. Syria agreed to the cease-fire shortly afterward.

Unfortunately, the cease-fire agreement did not bring an immediate end to the fighting along the Suez Canal. For the next few days, the Egyptian armies struggled to wriggle free from the Israeli trap, while the Israelis sought to close it ever tighter. Finding himself in desperate circumstances, Sadat called on Moscow and Washington for assistance. The big powers eventually agreed to support the sending of a UN Emergency Force (UNEF) to the area. Meanwhile, Kissinger forced the Israelis to permit a supply convoy through to the entrapped Egyptian Third Army, which was in danger of starving. On October 28, representatives of Israel and Egypt met face to face at Kilometer 101 (which was 101 kilometers, or 57 miles, from Cairo) to discuss the specifics of the convoy. Two days later, it was rolling toward the Third Army. Another Arab-Israeli war had finally ended.

SHUTTLE DIPLOMACY
The 1973 war had been different from the past two conflicts. For the Israelis, it had cost far more in lives, mon-

ey, and material. The Arabs had been more powerful than ever. Israel had not only faced the armies of Egypt, Syria, and Jordan, but military contingents had also been sent from Morocco and Algeria. And money had been contributed to the Arab cause by Kuwait, Saudi Arabia, and the Arab Emirates. The Israelis simply could not continue to fight such long wars without eventually bleeding themselves white.

The Arabs had injected another element into the Middle East situation too. For the first time they had effectively used their oil as a weapon. At a meeting in Kuwait, while the Yom Kippur War was still in progress, the Arab oil-producing countries agreed to reduce their oil shipments to those nations who supported Israel, until the Israelis withdrew from the occupied territories they had taken in the '67 war. These nations included Canada, the United States, and countries in western Europe. Eventually the U.S. was placed under a total embargo. The action taken by the oil producers was a serious blow to the industrialized nations of the West, who depended on Arab oil. As a result, they began to place increasing pressure on Israel to come to terms with the Arabs.

It was against this international backdrop that Secretary of State Kissinger set about trying to achieve an agreement between Israel and its Arab opponents. His aims were to achieve a broader peace settlement in the Middle East, without jeopardizing Israeli security, and lift the Arab oil embargo. But time was of the essence. A new conflict could erupt at any moment between Egyptian and Israeli forces along the Suez Canal. And the Arabs would continue their oil boycott unless Kissinger could prove that he was able to effectively argue their case and persuade Israel to withdraw from the occupied territories.

In his meetings with Mrs. Meir, however, Kissinger found her unwilling to withdraw from any of the territory which had been paid for in Jewish blood. This, she believed, was not the way to safeguard Israel's security and achieve peace. Mrs. Meir was also initially unprepared to loosen the Israeli grip on the Egyptian armies. Only after a great deal of negotiating, did Kissinger finally succeed in working out an agreement between Israel and Egypt. It called for Israel to permit the trapped Egyptian army to continue receiving supplies and for Egypt to return Israeli prisoners.

At this point, efforts to reach a broader Israeli-Egyptian agreement reached an impasse. Kissinger then obtained support from the USSR and some of the Arab states to convene a conference at Geneva, Switzerland, to continue the discussions. The conference, which opened in December 1973, was attended by representatives of the Soviet Union, Egypt, Jordan, Israel, and the United States. The Syrians decided to stay away. Although the conference failed to achieve a diplomatic breakthrough, at least Israel and the Arab states sat down together in the same room. This, in itself, was an accomplishment.

Following the breakdown of the conference, Egypt and Israel now decided to continue negotiations on their own, working through Kissinger as an intermediary. In Washington Kissinger met with Moshe Dayan who presented a proposal for a partial Israeli withdrawal in the Sinai. Jerusalem had decided that the time had come to accept a wider settlement. Pressure from the U.S. was continuing; in addition, Arab forces were daily growing stronger, and clashes had broken out repeatedly along the Suez Canal.

Following his meeting with Dayan, Kissinger flew to Cairo where he met President Sadat. Over the past few months relations between Sadat and Washington had improved greatly, following assurances from Kissinger that the Egyptian army would not be allowed to starve and that Israel would eventually withdraw in the Sinai. Sadat found that Dayan's proposal was similar to one of his own, which Kissinger then took on to Jerusalem.

Here he conferred with Israeli leaders and tried to narrow the areas of disagreement between the two sides. Once again, Kissinger flew back to Egypt and another conference with Sadat. During these few days in January 1974, shuttle diplomacy came into its own.

Finally, an agreement was reached and later signed by Egyptians and Israelis on January 18, at Kilometer 101. It called for Israeli forces to leave the west bank of the Suez Canal and withdraw to a position 12 miles (19 km) from the east bank. (See map, p. 49.) Along this line the Israelis would maintain a limited force. The Egyptians could advance to the east side of the canal where they too would be permitted to station a limited force. In between the two armies would be a demilitarized zone patrolled by UN troops. In a separate statement, which was addressed to the U.S. and not part of the agreement with Israel, Egypt also committed itself to open the Suez Canal, which had been closed in the 1967 war.

Following the Egyptian-Israeli agreement, Kissinger attempted to negotiate a settlement between Israel and Syria. This proved far more difficult, in part because of the enormous bitterness on both sides. Not until the end of May was a cease-fire agreement finally signed. It called for Israeli withdrawal approximately to the prewar lines and for Syria to remain east of these lines. A UN buffer zone was established between the two nations.

Israel and the Arab states had taken the first small step toward peace, but Kissinger hoped he could persuade them to go further. The secretary of state tried to convince the Israeli government to accept a withdrawal agreement along the Jordanian border similar to those governing the Suez Canal and the Golan Heights. But there was strong resistance to this proposal, for many Israelis regarded the West Bank as part of their ancient homeland.

Nevertheless, the Israeli government did express its willingness to undertake a further withdrawal in the Sinai. In return, it wanted Egypt to agree to end the state of war between the two countries. But Sadat was unwilling to do this unless Israel returned all the occupied territories. He also demanded that the Israelis give up more of the Sinai than they were prepared to relinquish. Kissinger was unable to bring the two sides together, and the negotiations eventually broke down.

Then in June 1975, Sadat announced his reopening of the Suez Canal. In response to this effort at improving relations, the Israelis pulled back further from the canal. Negotiations between Israel and Egypt, with Dr. Kissinger working as an intermediary, began again. Eventually, in September, another agreement was signed. Under its terms, Israel withdrew to a position in the Sinai east of the Gidi and Mitla passes. These two strategic areas would not be controlled by the UN. However, the United States agreed to operate monitoring devices within the passes which would serve as an early warning system in case of attack. Although Egypt did not specifically say that it would end the state of belligerency, it did "undertake not to resort to the threat or use of force or military blockade." Israeli cargos were also permitted through the Suez Canal.

The peace process had taken another important step forward.

6

Sadat, Begin, and Carter

The second Sinai Agreement of 1975 would not mark an end to the peace process; the leaders of Egypt and Israel had too large a stake in its continuation. President Sadat needed peace so he could rebuild Egypt's shaky economy, which had been further strained by the Yom Kippur War. Without the prospect of another war, he could reduce the size of his standing army and channel more money into domestic programs to improve the lives of his people. But Sadat believed that Egypt's economic recovery could be achieved only with assistance from western Europe and the United States. Their money and expertise were essential to expanding Egyptian industry and developing new agricultural projects. Yet Sadat knew that he could attract Western capital only in an atmosphere of peace.

Israeli leaders also seemed interested in continuing negotiations. In 1976, Prime Minister Yitzhak Rabin, who had replaced Golda Meir, had told Henry Kissinger that he was willing to undertake a further Israeli withdrawal in the Sinai if Egypt would end the state of war between the two countries. The following year, however, a sudden change occurred in Israeli politics which seemed to call into question Israel's desire for peace.

Ever since the founding of the state of Israel the Labor party had dominated the political scene. Labor and its allies held a majority of seats in the Knesset and, under the parliamentary system, selected the prime minister. The parliamentary elections of 1977 were different. Amid charges of incompetence and corruption, Labor lost at the polls. The new prime minister was Menachem Begin, who headed a coalition of rightist political parties. During the election campaign, Begin had made clear that he intended to hold on to the Israeli occupied territories. This did not seem to indicate a willingness to continue with the peace process.

But, in fact, Begin was far more conciliatory and ready to compromise than he may have appeared. As foreign minister he appointed Moshe Dayan, who had taken a moderate position on Israeli withdrawal from the Sinai. Through various diplomatic channels, including a meeting with Rumanian President Ceausescu, the new prime minister had indicated a willingness to be flexible on the Sinai. As later negotiations would show, Begin was prepared to withdraw from Egyptian territory, as long as he could retain Judea and Samaria (the West Bank land that had belonged to Jordan before the Six Day War). He regarded these biblical regions as integral parts of Israel.

By withdrawing from the Sinai, the Israelis would be abandoning a considerable investment. Since the 1967 war, they had developed oil fields in the desert and built huge military installations at tremendous cost. The Israelis had also established large settlements in the Sinai as well as along the West Bank. (See map, p. 49.) In these settlements Israeli citizens had built their homes and helped their government strengthen its control over the occupied territories.

In Washington the new administration of President

Jimmy Carter was proposing a Middle East settlement very different from the one Begin wanted. Carter wanted a comprehensive peace agreement that would include Israeli withdrawal from all the occupied territories and the establishment of a Palestinian "entity," or homeland, on the West Bank and the Gaza Strip. This was much farther than the Israelis wanted to go. They regarded any type of "entity" as leading to the creation of an independent Palestinian state. This, they believed, would be dominated by the PLO, whose leader, Yasir Arafat, had vowed to destroy Israel.

To achieve a comprehensive settlement, the Carter plan also called for eventually reopening talks at Geneva with representatives of the USSR, the Arab states, and the Palestinians. But in November 1977, President Sadat surprised everyone with his decision to fly to Jerusalem. Sadat's visit, in effect, bypassed Geneva. The Egyptian president also hoped it might lead to a speedy peace agreement with the Israelis.

In his speech before the Knesset, Sadat outlined the terms he had in mind for this agreement. Israel, he said, should be allowed to live in "security and safety" with its Arab neighbors. But, in return, Sadat expected the Israelis to pay a stiff price: he wanted them to withdraw from the occupied territories and recognize the Palestinians' right to "statehood."

Sadat had called on Israel to make substantially the same concessions that the Carter administration had proposed. These proposals would now be debated over and over during the long and difficult negotiations that were to follow.

THE NEGOTIATIONS BEGIN

A few weeks after Sadat's visit to Jerusalem, peace talks began in Cairo between representatives of Israel, Egypt, and the United States. Very little was accomplished at these initial meetings, except that the Israelis had their first exposure to the Egyptian people. Meanwhile, important diplomatic efforts had been under way in other locations. Following his return from Israel, Sadat had tried to enlist the support of King Hussein for a plan that called for Jordanian takeover of the West Bank. But the king was reluctant to commit himself, fearing the negative reaction of Syria and other Arab states, and the PLO.

As talks were about to start in Cairo, Prime Minister Begin was flying to Washington to present his own peace plan to President Carter. The plan included limited self-government for the Palestinians on the West Bank and Gaza. Palestinian officials would have control over economic and cultural affairs, while the all-important areas of security and public order would remain in the hands of the Israelis. In Sinai, Begin envisioned a two-stage Israeli withdrawal that would not be finished until the year 2000. Thus, the prime minister's plan included important concessions, but it fell far short of President Carter's proposals.

A few days later, meetings took place in Egypt between Sadat and Israeli Defense Minister Ezer Weizman. As Weizman explains in his memoirs, he and Sadat had begun a friendship when the Egyptian president came to Jerusalem. During the days and weeks ahead, Sadat would often express his opinions to Weizman and rely on him to transmit them to other Israeli officials. At these initial meetings Sadat repeated his demands that Israel must withdraw from the occupied territories. Weizman had hoped to find Sadat more flexible. The defense minister wanted to retain Israel's Rafah settlements along the Gaza Strip as well as some strategic airfields in the Sinai. But Sadat insisted that Israel must totally evacuate Egyptian territory.

On December 25, Begin and Sadat conferred at Ismalia, the Egyptian city located along the Suez Canal. Both men agreed that their representatives should continue discussions in Cairo and at the same time begin a new series of talks in Jerusalem to discuss other issues.

Otherwise, the conference accomplished nothing. Begin and Sadat were still too far apart.

Seeking to change Sadat's position on the Sinai, the Israeli government decided on a more radical course of action. They began to erect "token" settlements consisting of only a few buildings. The reasoning was that if Sadat demanded the removal of these settlements, the Israelis would comply. But, in return for this gesture, they would expect Sadat to allow them to retain the Rafah settlements. This decision by the Begin government was strongly opposed by Weizman, as well as many other Israelis who feared it would jeopardize the peace process.

In Cairo, Sadat was furious. He threatened to burn the Israeli settlements in the Sinai if they were not evacuated. Begin responded by calling the Egyptian president "Nero."

This atmosphere of increasing bitterness prompted Sadat to fly to Washington in February, 1978 for a meeting with President Carter. The Egyptian leader had hoped that his visit to Jerusalem would result in an early agreement with the Israelis. But each day that agreement seemed further away, and Sadat was forced to withstand increasing censure and hostility throughout much of the Arab world. To rescue his position, Sadat needed to break the stalemate with Israel, and he knew that only the American president might have the power and willingness to do it.

Carter had opposed Israel's "token" settlements in the Sinai, and his proposals for peace seemed much closer to Sadat's than to Begin's. In March, when Ezer Weizman met Carter in Washington, the Israeli defense minister reported that Carter had praised Sadat for his flexibility. Carter now expected the same thing from the Israelis, Weizman said.

But there seemed to be no spirit of compromise in Jerusalem. Instead, the Begin government announced that more Jewish settlements would be erected along the

[70]

West Bank. This provoked a highly critical response from the Carter administration.

Meanwhile, at the end of March, Weizman conferred once again with Sadat in what proved to be an extraordinary meeting. According to Weizman, the Egyptian president said he was not interested in a Palestinian state on the West Bank and Gaza, but he did want to give the Palestinians some degree of autonomy, or self-rule. At the same time, Sadat recognized that Israel must protect its own security in the region. The Egyptian leader now seemed to be moving toward the Israeli position on the Palestinian question. But the very next day, Sadat announced that he had changed his mind and withdrew the proposal.

As the stalemate between Egypt and Israel continued, Begin's popularity inside his own country began to ebb. Many Israelis believed he was too unyielding and that peace was slipping away.

Sadat was no longer willing to meet with Begin. Instead, the Egyptian president summoned Weizman for yet another meeting, this time in Salzburg, Austria. Their talks were held in July, just before the foreign ministers of Egypt, Israel, and the United States were due to meet in London. Sadat believed this conference would be a failure, and he wanted to maintain his own private channel of communications with the Israeli defense minister.

According to Weizman, the Egyptian leader wanted Israel to make a "gesture," as he had done by coming to Jerusalem. What Sadat asked for, specifically, was the immediate return of another part of the Sinai. Once again, the Egyptian president emphasized that Israel must eventually withdraw from the occupied territories. But he was prepared to allow an Israeli military presence on the West Bank and the Gaza Strip. The Palestinians, he said, must be allowed some self-government; however, Sadat did not envision a Palestinian state.

Unfortunately, Sadat's proposals were distinctly dif-

[71]

ferent from those presented by the Egyptian foreign minister in London. He took a much tougher position on full Israeli withdrawal from the occupied territories and the rights of the Palestinians. In response, Begin refused to give Sadat the "gesture" he wanted. The Egyptian president then retaliated by ordering the Israeli peace negotiators in Cairo to depart for home.

The peace process seemed to have reached a dead end.

A MEETING AT CAMP DAVID

It was President Jimmy Carter who rescued the peace talks and gave them new life. Carter invited Begin and Sadat to meet with him in the United States and continue the negotiations. In September the three leaders went to Camp David, the presidential retreat tucked away in the Maryland hills. Separate cabins had been assigned to Sadat and his entourage, Begin and his advisors (who included Dayan and Weizman), and the U.S. negotiating team, headed by Carter.

On the first evening, Carter met with Begin, and they discussed the various issues that still divided Israel and Egypt. In the course of their conversations, Carter emphasized the importance of reaching an agreement during the conference if the peace process were to be saved.

The next day Carter and Begin listened as Sadat presented his conditions for peace. These included Israeli withdrawal from the occupied territories, including east Jerusalem; provision for the Palestinians to eventually establish a national "entity"; and compensation by the Israelis for all the destruction which their armies had caused in the occupied lands. These were the toughest demands Sadat had ever made, and the Israelis found them totally unacceptable.

Over the next few days, additional meetings took place between Carter, Sadat, and Begin, but they accomplished nothing. Meanwhile, Carter and his team—

including Secretary of State Cyrus Vance and National Security Advisor Zbignew Brzezinski—tried to bring the two sides closer together. It was no use. After a week of meetings, the conference seemed about to collapse.

Dayan now talked of going home. Sadat was also pessimistic about the chances of achieving a breakthrough. He called Weizman in for another meeting and, according to the defense minister, confessed that "my mood is not good." Once again, Weizman tried to persuade Sadat that Israel should be allowed to keep its airfields and the Rafah settlements in Sinai, but Sadat refused.

By this time Weizman had become convinced that the Sinai held the key to peace. For many months he had believed that Sadat would be willing to accept some small concession on the Palestinian question to save face in the Arab world. But the Sinai was Egyptian territory, and Sadat would not be content until he controlled all of it. Following his own meeting with the Egyptian president, at Camp David, Dayan too had become convinced of this.

Carter, meantime, had also begun to concentrate on the Sinai issue. The president emphasized in his talks with Weizman and Dayan that Israel must be willing to withdraw from Sinai. The two cabinet ministers then conferred with Begin. He had come to Camp David hoping to hang on to the Rafah settlements and the airfields. But the prime minister now realized that this would be impossible if he wanted an agreement with Egypt. His decision was made easier by the fact that the United States had earlier agreed to build new airfields for Israel in the Negev.

Finally on September 17, 1978, after almost two weeks of exhausting negotiations, the leaders of Israel, Egypt, and the United States stood before the television cameras in Washington. Before a worldwide audience, Sadat and Begin signed the agreements that had been reached at Camp David while President Carter acted as

[73]

a witness. The Camp David accords were in no small measure due to his stubborn persistence and thorough knowledge of the complex issues in the Middle East.

Two agreements were signed as a result of Camp David. The first, called a "Framework for Peace in the Middle East," dealt directly with the Palestinian question. According to the Framework, Egypt, Israel and Jordan would discuss the establishment of an elected self-governing authority in the West Bank and Gaza. Eventually, the Israelis would remove their military government and restrict their military units to specified areas; the Palestinians would be given "full autonomy" (self-government). Finally, representatives of Israel, Egypt, Jordan, and the Palestinian people would decide upon the final status of the West Bank and Gaza.

Although the Framework represented some concessions by the Israelis, it did not call for the establishment of a Palestinian state. Israel was also permitted to maintain a military presence in the occupied areas.

In addition to the Palestinian question, the Framework took up Israel's relations with other Arab countries. It referred to peace agreements that might eventually be concluded between Israel and Lebanon, Jordan, and Syria. These were to be guided by the same "principle and provisions" as the Framework involving Israel and Egypt.

The second document that came out of Camp David was called a "Framework for the Conclusion of a Peace Treaty between Egypt and Israel." This included a stage by stage withdrawal of all Israeli settlements and armed forces from the Sinai. After an interim stage of withdrawal, diplomatic relations would be established between Cairo and Jerusalem. Israel would also receive free access to the Suez Canal, the Straits of Tiran, and the Gulf of Aqaba.

While the Israelis had won concessions on Palestine, Sadat had achieved all that he wanted in Sinai. At the same time, he had obtained an agreement that seemed

[74]

more than just a separate peace with Israel. It mentioned full autonomy for the Palestinians as well as eventual peace treaties with the other Arab states. These elements were crucial because the other Arab leaders would have denounced a separate peace as a betrayal.

FINALLY, A PEACE TREATY

The Camp David accords were considered only a preliminary agreement which would lead to a formal peace treaty within the next three months. To negotiate the final terms of that treaty, Israeli and Egyptian representatives began meeting in Washington during October. Observers generally believed the negotiating sessions would run smoothly because there were just a few points that remained to be decided. But as the talks continued, more problems arose. The Israelis insisted on their right to establish new settlements along the West Bank. In fact, Prime Minister Begin had even gone so far as to declare that this territory was Israeli land.

President Sadat now began to look more and more like a man who had abandoned the Palestinians and the other Arab states for a separate peace with Israel. No one in the Arab world supported him. King Hussein refused to join the peace process, and Saudi Arabia, considered a moderate Arab state, also refused to endorse it. Finally, in November, the Arab leaders decided to take joint action against Sadat. At a meeting in Baghdad, they vowed to end diplomatic relations with Egypt if he signed a treaty with Israel.

Faced with this unpleasant situation, Sadat now began to toughen Egypt's position in the peace negotiations. He demanded from the Israelis a firm commitment to Palestinian autonomy by a specified date. Sadat also wanted to make sure that this peace treaty would not prevent Egypt from carrying out its defensive alliances with other Arab states if they were attacked by Israel.

Begin refused Sadat's demands regarding the Palestinians. In turn, the Israeli prime minister demanded

[75]

that since he was giving up important oil fields in the Sinai, Egypt must assure Israel a continuing supply of oil. For months the talks dragged on, as Israel and Egypt were unable to resolve their differences. The peace treaty, which had seemed so close at Camp David, now appeared to be drifting away.

Once again, it was Jimmy Carter who finally brought the two sides together. In Washington he persuaded Begin that a goal of one year should be set for completing negotiations leading to the Palestinian self-governing authority mentioned at Camp David. Then Carter flew to Cairo where he obtained Sadat's agreement on this formula. The Egyptian president also accepted Carter's compromise proposal on the relationship between an Egyptian-Israeli agreement and Egypt's treaties with other Arab states.

Conducting his own brand of shuttle diplomacy, Carter traveled on to Jerusalem, expecting to find the Israelis set to sign a treaty. Instead, he discovered that some points which Sadat had insisted on still had to be resolved before the Israelis were satisfied. Carter had placed his prestige on the line by coming to the Middle East. Now it appeared that some final sticking points might prevent a peace treaty from being signed. But at the last moment, these issues were resolved following meetings between Moshe Dayan and Secretary of State Cyrus Vance, who had accompanied President Carter. An Egyptian-Israeli peace treaty became a reality; it was signed on March 26, 1979.

The treaty contained many of the same provisions as the Camp David accords. It called for "the establishment of a just, comprehensive and lasting peace in the Middle East. . . . " A phased withdrawal of Israeli armed forces from the Sinai was to take place over three years, with diplomatic relations to be established between Egypt and Israel after an interim phase. There was also an annex that included economic and trade relations,

[76]

cultural relations, and freedom of movement between the two countries. Separate from the treaty was a joint letter to President Carter signed by Sadat and Begin. In it they agreed to proceed with negotiations leading to full autonomy for the West Bank and the Gaza Strip, but the timetable for autonomy remained somewhat vague.

The new Israeli-Egyptian peace treaty was a significant agreement not only for what it did, but also for what it did not, accomplish. As a result of the treaty, Egypt became the first Arab state to establish diplomatic relations with Israel and recognize its right to exist. Israel had thus broken the alliance of Arab states that threatened it with annihilation. Sadat's Arab critics contended that he had also given the Israelis a much freer hand to pursue their aggressive policies. With its southern border now more secure, Israel might feel less restrained in its dealings with other Arab states. But Sadat needed the peace treaty in order to secure U.S. aid and investment, which could help his economy along the road to recovery. And he was prepared to pay the price: ostracism by the other Arab states.

While the peace treaty had clearly defined the new relationship between Egypt and Israel, it left another issue unresolved. This was the status of the Palestinians. The treaty had been purposely vague about the step-by-step process that would lead to full autonomy for the West Bank and the Gaza Strip. Autonomy also fell far short of an independent state, which was the dream of many Palestinians. A solution to the Palestinian problem was crucial if Israel ever hoped to establish peaceful relations with the other Arab states. Otherwise the Middle East could easily dissolve in conflict once again.

7

Will There Be Peace?

As expected, Sadat and his new peace treaty were denounced in many parts of the Arab world. The Arab League took swift and decisive action. On March 27, 1979, only a day after the treaty was signed, the League announced that its members would sever diplomatic relations with Egypt. Even the moderate Arab states, such as Jordan and Saudi Arabia, endorsed the decision despite intensive efforts by Sadat and the Carter administration to enlist their support for a treaty. A role for King Hussein had even been envisioned in the Palestinian autonomy talks, but he refused to join them.

Nevertheless, the peace process continued. In April, Prime Minister Begin journeyed to Cairo for a meeting with President Sadat. As a gesture of friendship, the prime minister announced that the first part of the Sinai, including El-Arish, would be returned to Egypt ahead of schedule. During May, the two leaders proclaimed the opening of the borders between their countries. Then, at the beginning of 1980, Israel completed its evacuation of two-thirds of the Sinai. Following the withdrawal, Egypt and Israel established formal diplomatic relations and exchanged ambassadors.

The smooth transfer of the Sinai was in marked contrast to the problems which developed over the Palestinian autonomy issue. The autonomy talks, which had been called for in the peace agreements, opened in May at Beersheba in the Israeli Negev. The talks included representatives of Egypt, Israel, and the United States. But they were held without the Palestinians, who would not participate unless they received the permission of the PLO. But PLO leader Yasir Arafat* refused to join the peace process. Regarding the treaty as a sellout, Arafat continued to call for the destruction of Israel and the establishment of a Palestinian state. The Israelis, on their part, refused to recognize the PLO or deal with Arafat.

There was enough friction at the autonomy talks even without Palestinian participation. All the issues that had separated Egypt and Israel in the past—and were sidestepped at Camp David—now resurfaced. Both sides strongly disagreed over the type of self-governing authority to be established on the West Bank and Gaza. The Israelis wanted to severely restrict its autonomy, fearing that too much would eventually lead to the creation of an independent state. The Egyptians, on the other hand, pushed for broader autonomy. Sadat was well aware that he had to silence his critics in the Arab world who were accusing him of betraying the Palestinians. He needed to demonstrate that the peace process would work so Egypt could regain its position of Arab leadership. Sadat even went so far as to renew his call for Palestinian self-determination, which the Israelis interpreted to mean an independent state.

The Egyptian president also demanded that the Israelis remove their settlements from the occupied territories and withdraw from them, including East Jerusalem. In defiance of Sadat, the Israeli Knesset declared the

---

* Arafat, who had been head of al-Fatah, one of the most powerful groups in the PLO, was named chairman of the PLO in 1969.

undivided city of Jerusalem as the capital of Israel. At this point, the Egyptian president decided not to continue the automony talks. Although they were later resumed, the talks achieved little. The peace agreements had mentioned a goal of one year for the completion of negotiations leading to the election of a self-governing authority in the occupied territories. But that deadline came and passed with the election no closer.

The failure of the autonomy talks was due in part to a decision by Prime Minister Begin to expand existing Israeli settlements along the West Bank and build new ones. This decision was severely criticized by Sadat as well as President Carter, both of whom regarded it as an effort to increase Israeli control over the occupied territories. The Palestinians also resented these settlements because they were built in areas with a heavy population of Arabs and on land which had often been confiscated from them by the Israeli government.

The settlement policy created deep divisions within the Israeli cabinet too. While Agricultural Minister Ariel Sharon championed the program, Moshe Dayan and Ezer Weizman were strongly opposed because it seemed to jeopardize the peace process. Both men eventually resigned in protest over Begin's approach to carrying out the treaty agreements, Dayan in 1979 and Weizman in 1980. Dayan submitted his own proposal for the future of the West Bank and Gaza. It included withdrawing the Israeli military administration from the cities; leaving armed forces only in strategic areas to protect Israeli security; building settlements to support the army; and ending the confiscation of privately held Arab lands.

But the Begin government seemed unwilling to follow a policy of greater moderation. Instead, Israeli occupation of the West Bank and Gaza Strip intensified, leading to protests and riots by the Palestinians during 1981 and '82.

[80]

AN UNCERTAIN FUTURE

On October 6, 1981, President Anwar Sadat was assassinated in Cairo. The assassination occurred while Sadat was watching a military parade held to commemorate the Egyptian crossing of the Suez Canal in the 1973 war.

The death of Sadat created uncertainty about the future of the peace process. His successor, Vice President Hosni Mubarak, was a little-known leader, just as Sadat had been when he succeeded Nasser in 1970. But Mubarak reassured Washington and Jerusalem of his intention to abide by the peace treaty. And on April 25, 1982, the Israelis withdrew from the final portion of the Sinai which was returned to Egypt. (See map, p. 49.) This area was patrolled by a multinational peace-keeping force made up of troops and observers from eleven countries, creating a buffer zone between Israel and Egypt.

The final pullout was marked by fireworks over the Nile, but in Israel there seemed little cause for celebration. Many Israelis wondered whether the Egyptians really would keep the peace now that they had regained their land. Others felt sorrow for the Israeli settlers who had been forced to give up their homes in the Sinai when it was returned.

While Israeli citizens tried to adjust to the mixed blessings of peace with Egypt, they faced a far more dangerous situation along their northern border. Inside Lebanon the IDF was locked in a bitter struggle with the PLO and the armed forces of Syria. To understand how this conflict arose, a little background on the Lebanese problem might prove helpful.

The country of Lebanon is divided between Christians and Muslims, who have lived together in an uneasy partnership. According to a formula worked out years before, both groups shared political power, although friction often developed between their leaders. Into this atmosphere came the PLO in 1970-71, after it was driv-

[81]

en out of Jordan. Shifting its base of operations to Lebanon, the PLO took control of the Palestinian refugee camps and used them as staging areas for raids against Israel. In return, the Israelis staged reprisal attacks in Lebanon.

The presence of the PLO and the Israeli reprisals further strained relations between Christians and Muslims. While the PLO generally received support from the Muslims, it was opposed by the Chrstians, who feared the guerrillas might upset the delicate political balance inside Lebanon. Nevertheless, the PLO was permitted to remain.

Gradually, the political situation in Lebanon deteriorated, and during 1975 a civil war broke out between Christian groups and Muslim leftists who were supported by the PLO. Bloody fighting erupted around Beirut, the Lebanese capital, and in other parts of the country. From across the border, the war was closely watched by the Syrians, who viewed it as a threat to their own political stability. Finally, Syria intervened militarily and forced the two sides to accept a cease-fire.

But the fighting had ended only temporarily. New clashes soon occurred in southern Lebanon between the PLO and the Christians, who had begun receiving support from Israel. The Israelis believed that an alliance with the Christians might prove useful in defeating the PLO. The Lebanese civil war was slowly becoming part of the broader conflict between Israel and the Arabs.

In 1978, following a PLO attack which took the lives of many Israeli adults and children, Jerusalem ordered an invasion of Lebanon. Israeli armed forces destroyed many PLO strongholds and occupied an area in the south bordering the Litani River. Eventually, the Israelis withdrew from this area and were replaced by a UN peacekeeping force. But instead of handing over all the territory to the UN the Israelis gave a 6-mile (9.7-km) stretch along the border to their allies, the Christians, who were expected to create a buffer zone.

[82]

The presence of the UN did not bring peace to the region. PLO attacks and Israeli reprisal raids continued. In another development, fighting had broken out in Beirut in 1978 between Syrian armed forces and Christian militia groups. The Israelis, who regarded the Syrian army in Lebanon as a threat to their security, decided to provide air and naval support to the Christians. Repeated clashes erupted during 1979 and 1980 between Syrian and Israeli jets in the skies over Lebanon, further widening the Lebanese conflict. At the same time, Israeli and Christian troops battled PLO units who were being assisted by the Syrians. As the crisis escalated in 1981, strenuous attempts were under way to end it. Finally, due to the efforts of the United States and others, a cease-fire was arranged between Israel and the PLO along the border in southern Lebanon.

But the level of violence was reduced only temporarily. In June 1982, Israeli forces invaded Lebanon to strike at the PLO. According to Prime Minister Begin, the Israeli objective was to destroy the PLO bases located within a 25-mile-wide (40-km) area in southern Lebanon. From these bases the Palestinian guerrillas had shelled Israeli settlements across the border. But after the PLO had been removed, Israeli forces continued their advance northward. They destroyed the remaining PLO strongholds located in various Lebanese towns and cities, including parts of Beirut. During the fighting, thousands of innocent civilians lost their lives, and many more were left homeless. Inside Beirut the PLO forces were saved from destruction by the Israelis at only the very last minute. Under the terms of an agreement worked out by the parties involved in the war, PLO troops were transported from Beirut to safety in eight other Arab states.

Although the military power of the PLO had ended, the violence was not yet over for Beirut's Palestinian civilians. On September 14, 1982, the president-elect of Lebanon, a Christian named Bashir Gemayel was assas-

[83]

sinated when his headquarters was bombed. In retaliation, members of a Christian group infiltrated Palestinian civilian camps and killed hundreds of men, women, and children over a two-day period. Because Israeli soldiers were guarding the camps at the time, in an effort to prevent bloodshed, the role of the Israeli army in the massacre was immediately called into question. Investigations that followed reached the highest levels of the Israeli government.

In the Middle East peace still remains more a dream than a reality. For a time, Camp David raised expectations that a broad framework of peace might be possible, but so far this hasn't occurred, because the issues that divided Israel and the Arab states in the past continue to divide them today. Arab leaders, with the notable exception of the Egyptians, refuse to acknowledge Israel's right to exist. This hostility, combined with Israel's feeling of insecurity, can only breed renewed conflict. Israel, on the other hand, refuses to acknowledge the claims of the Palestinians. Yet, to many Arabs, this is the crux of the Middle East problem. The issues of Israeli security and Palestinian rights are at the core of the current war in Lebanon.

To break the continuing cycle of war in the Middle East will require a new series of tough negotiations. But something more is needed. Arab and Israeli leaders must be willing to break through the psychological barriers that presently keep them apart. In short, they will need the same spirit of peace and reconciliation that guided Anwar Sadat on his courageous journey to Jerusalem.

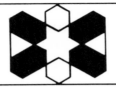

For Further Reading

Archer, Jules. *Legacy of the Desert*. Boston: Little, Brown, 1976.

Ben-Gurion, David. *Israel, A Personal History*. Tel Aviv: American Israel Publishing Co., 1971.

Cohen, Aharon. *Israel and the Arab World*. New York: Funk and Wagnalls, 1970.

Dayan, Moshe. *Breakthrough: A Personal Account of the Egypt-Israel Peace Negotiations*. New York: Knopf, 1981.

_____. *The Story of My Life*. New York: William Morrow, 1976.

Dimbleby, Jonathan. *The Palestinians*. New York: Quartet Books, 1979.

el-Sadat, Anwar. *In Search of Identity*. New York: Harper and Row, 1978.

Haber, Eitan, et al. *The Year of the Dove*. New York: Bantam Books, 1979.

Khalidi, Walid. *Conflict and Violence in Lebanon: Confrontation in the Middle East*. Cambridge, Mass.: Center for International Affairs, Harvard University, 1979.

Khouri, Fred. *The Arab-Israeli Dilemma.* Syracuse, N.Y.: Syracuse University Press, 1968.

Kissinger, Henry M. *The Years of Upheaval.* Boston: Little, Brown, 1982.

Neff, Donald. *Warriors at Suez.* New York: Simon and Schuster, 1981.

Nutting, Anthony. *Nasser.* New York: E.P. Dutton, 1972.

Sachar, Howard. *Egypt and Israel.* New York: Richard Marek, 1981.

Safran, Nadav. *Israel the Embattled Ally.* Cambridge, Mass.: Harvard University Press, 1978.

Said, Edward. *The Question of Palestine.* Times Books, 1979.

Schmidt, Dana A. *Armageddon in the Middle East.* New York: The N.Y. Times, 1974.

Weizman, Ezer. *The Battle for Peace.* New York: Bantam Books, 1981.

Magazines and Newspapers: *Current History; Foreign Affairs; The New York Times; U.S. News and World Report; Time* magazine.

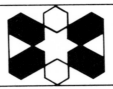

Index

Abdullah, King of Jordan, 25

Abraham, Old Testament patriarch, 4

Al-Assad, Hafez, President of Syria, 57

Alexander II, Tsar of Russia, 7

Al-Fatah, radical Palestinian group, 39–41, 54–55, 79

Al-Rahman Pasha, Abd, Arab League Secretary-General, 19

Arab-Israeli war (1948–1949), 18–21

Arab League, 18–19, 39, 78

Arab Legion of Transjordan, 19–21

Arab oil embargo, 62

Arafat, Yasir, leader of al-Fatah, 39–40, 55–56, 68, 79

Auto-emancipation: A Warning of a Russian Jew to His Brethren (Pinsker), 7

Autonomy, Palestinian, issue of, 68, 74–77, 79–80

Balfour, Arthur, British Foreign Secretary, 10

Balfour Declaration (1917), 11, 13

Bar-Lev, Chaim, Israeli Chief of Staff, 53

Begin, Menachem, Israeli Prime Minister, 1–2, 15, 67–77, 78, 80, 83

Ben-Gurion, David, Israeli Prime Minister, 17, 20, 26, 30, 31, 34, 36

British role in the Middle East, 10–16, 21, 28–29, 32–37, 45

Brzezinski, Zbignew, United States Security Advisor, 73

Camp David negotiations (1978), 72–75, 83–84

Carter, Jimmy, President of the United States, 67–69, 70–74, 76–77, 78, 80

Ceausescu, Nicolae, President of Rumania, 1–2, 67
Cyrus the Great, King of Persia, 5

David, King of the Israelites, 4
Dayan, Moshe, Israeli Cabinet Minister, 20, 29–31, 33, 35–36, 45–46, 53, 54–55, 59, 63, 67, 72–73, 76, 80
De Gaulle, Charles, President of France, 45
Dreyfus, Alfred, French officer, 8

Eban, Abba, Israeli Foreign Minister, 45
Eden, Anthony, British Prime Minister, 34, 36
Egypt, role of in Middle East conflicts, 19–21, 23, 27–29, 30–37, 41–51, 76–77. *See also* Peace negotiations in the Middle East
Egypt and Israel (Sacher), 30
Egyptian-Israeli peace treaty (1979), 76–77
El-Sadat, Anwar, President of Egypt, 1–2, 33, 43, 56–59, 60–61, 63–64, 65, 66, 68–77, 78–81, 84
Eshkol, Levi, Israeli Prime Minister, 41, 44–45

Farouk, King of Egypt, 27
Fatah. *See* Al-Fatah
Ferdinand, Franz, Archduke of Austria, 10
First Zionist Congress (1896), 8
French role in the Middle East, 11–12, 31, 33–37, 45

Guerrilla movement, Palestinian Arab, 18, 29–30, 39–41, 54–56, 81–83

Haganah, Jewish military force, 13–14, 15, 19–21. *See also* Israeli Defense Force
Hassan II, King of Morocco, 1
Herzl, Theodor, Zionist leader, 8
History of the Jews, 3–16
Hussein, Sharif, Arab leader, 10, 11–12
Hussein, King of Jordan, 41, 43–44, 46–47, 55–56, 69, 74, 78

In Search of Identity (el-Sadat), 43
International interests in the Middle East: British, 10–16, 21, 28–29, 32–37, 45; French, 11–12, 31, 33–37, 45; Soviet, 30–31, 33, 42–43, 50, 52–53, 56–58, 60–61, 63; United Nations, 16, 18, 20–21, 23–24, 37, 41, 43, 47, 50–51, 61, 64, 82–83; United States, 32–33, 36, 37, 45, 50, 53, 60–61, 62–65, 67–69, 70–75, 79
Iraq, role of in Middle East conflicts, 19–20, 44, 60
Irgun, radical Zionist group, 15, 23
Israeli-Arab truce agreements (1949), 21
Israeli-Arab war (1948–1949), 18–21
Israeli declaration of independence (1948), 17–18

Israeli Defense Force (IDF), 26, 29–30. *See also* Haganah

Israeli-Egyptian peace treaty (1979), 76–77

Israeli invasion of Lebanon (1982), 81–83

Israeli occupation of Arab territory, 38–39, 54–55, 67, 70–71, 79–80. *See also* Sinai, Israeli transfer to Egypt

Jesus Christ, founder of Christianity, 3

Jews, history of, 3–16

Jordan, role of in Middle East conflicts, 19–21, 23, 30, 39, 41, 43–44, 46–48, 54–56, 60, 69

Kissinger, Henry, United States Secretary of State, 61, 62–65, 66

Lawrence, T. E., British officer, 10

Lebanon, Israeli invasion of (1982), 81–83

Lebanon, role of in Middle East conflicts, 19–20, 23, 55–56, 81–83

Meir, Golda, Israeli Prime Minister, 33, 36–37, 58–59, 62–63

Mohammed, Prophet of Islam, 3

Moses, leader of Israelites, 4

Mubarak, Hosni, President of Egypt, 81

Nasser, Gamal Abdel, President of Egypt, 28–33, 35, 36–37, 41–50, 52–53, 56

Nebuchadnezzar, King of Babylonia, 4

Nordan, Max, Zionist leader, 9

Occupation of Arab territory by Israel, 1, 38–39, 54–55, 67, 70–71, 79–80. *See also* Sinai, Israeli transfer to Egypt

Our Palestine, al-Fatah magazine, 40

Palestine, religious significance of, 3–5

Palestine Liberation Army, 18

Palestine Liberation Organization (PLO), 39, 68, 79, 81–83

Palestinian Arab: autonomy, 68, 74–77, 79–80; guerrilla movement, 18, 29–30, 39–41, 54–56, 81–83; refugees, 23–27, 55

Palestinian mandate, League of Nations, 12

Peace negotiations in the Middle East, 1–2, 21, 50–51, 61–79, 81, 83–84

Peres, Shimon, Israeli Director-General of Defense, 33

Pineau, Christian, French Foreign Minister, 34

Pinsker, Leon, Zionist leader, 7

Popular Front for the Liberation of Palestine (PFLP), 55

Question of Palestine, The (Said), 54

Rabin, Yitzhak, Israeli Prime Minister, 66
Rahman Pasha, Abd al-. *See* Al-Rahman Pasha, Abd
Refugees, Palestinian Arab, 23–27, 55, 83
Religious significance of Palestine, 3–5
Resolution 242, United Nations, 50–51
Rothschild, Baron Edmond de, Zionist, 8

Sacher, Howard M., 30
Sadat, Anwar el-. *See* El-Sadat, Anwar
Said, Edward, 54
Sharon, Ariel, Israeli Cabinet Minister, 80
Shuttle diplomacy, 61–65
Sinai, Israeli transfer to Egypt, 78–79, 81
Six Day war (1967), 38–51
Solomon, King of the Israelites, 4
Soviet role in the Middle East, 21, 30–31, 33, 42–43, 50, 52–53, 56–58, 60–61, 63
Stern Gang, radical Israeli group, 23
Suez Canal crisis (1956), 28–29, 32–37
Syria, role of in Middle East conflicts, 19–20, 23, 27, 39, 40–41, 43, 47, 48, 57, 60

Terrorists. *See* Guerilla movement, Palestinian Arab

Titus, Roman Emperor, 5

United Nations Resolution 242 (1967), 50–51
United Nations role in the Middle East, 16, 18, 20–21, 23–24, 37, 41, 43, 47, 50–51, 61, 64, 82–83
United States role in the Middle East, 32–33, 36, 37, 45, 50, 53, 60–61, 62–65, 67–69, 70–75, 79
U Thant, United Nations Secretary-General, 43

Vance, Cyrus, United States Secretary of State, 73, 76

Wars between Israel and the Arab states: (1948–1949) 18–21; (1956) 35–37; (1967) 38–51; (1973) 52–65; (1983) 81–83
Weizman, Chaim, Zionist leader, 11
Weizman, Ezer, Israeli Defense Minister, 69, 70–71, 72–73, 80
World War I, 10–12
World War II, 14–15

Yadin, Yigal, Israeli Chief of Staff, 26
Yom Kippur war (1973), 52–65

Zionism, 6–9